AF538254

FIVE KEYS TO EMOTIONAL ONENESS

THE EMOTIONAL DETOX SYSTEM

CELINA BELMARCE PINA PSY.D.

5 Keys To Emotional Oneness
The Emotional Detox System

Copyright © 2017 Celina Belmarce Pina Psy.D.

ISBN-13: 978-0-9987775-0-4

Published by: Healing Dialogues Publishing
New York, NY
http://www.healingdialogues.com

All Rights Reserved. No part of this book may be reproduced or transmitted in any form or by any means, electronic or mechanical, including photocopying, recording, or by an information storage and retrieval system - except by a reviewer who may quote brief passages in a review to be printed in a magazine or newspaper - without permission in writing from the publisher.

Printed in the United States of America

Cover Design © 2016 Fitzcarmel LaMarre
Book Layout: Training For the Kingdom

Dedication

To all those who have experienced pain
To all those who are journeying through preparation
To all those who are looking for their purpose
To all those who have a story to tell
………………….and to all the Belle's

TABLE OF CONTENTS

BOOK II — THE EMOTIONAL DETOX SYSTEM JOURNAL WORKBOOK

Acknowledgements

………to all those who made time to listen, who reached out without being asked, who called unexpectedly, who made time to provide unsolicited supports, and who focused on quality of time and relationship. I Thank You.

………to all those who, over the past 30 years, have trusted in my clinical abilities, who have believed in me and have helped in sustaining my clinical practice. To those who have returned as adults and brought their children, other family members, friends, and co-workers, For those who have come by to say hello and say thank you and for those who have returned just to stay emotionally healthy. I Thank You.

………to my loving daughter, Chantal, who has walked with me and supported all my efforts. To my mother, Rosie; and father, Eddie, who loved me unconditionally and always believed in me. To my grandparents, Henrequette and Venila who were my blanket and light of protection and love. A special thanks to, Venilia who was my mentor and role model. I Thank You……

………and most importantly; to Father God for with him all things are possible. I Praise and Glorify You.

Forward

Life will take you down a series of mountain and valley experiences. Along the way we can get bruised, battered, bewildered and broken. For most of us the luxury to self-reflect is lost in the busyness of life leaving remnants of unfinished business and old baggage along the way. Because life must go on, we carry this baggage oblivious of the weight. We carry it for so long until we no longer can distinguish what it feels like not to carry the weight. Because it becomes so much a part of our DNA we can be totally unaware of how this baggage impacts our relationships, our peace and our joy. Dr. Celina Belmarce Pina's book, *Five Keys to Emotional Oneness* takes you through a healing process that restores the authentic self. Enjoy the journey to wholeness.

Peace and Blessings,

Rev. Carol Dougherty-Steptoe

President,
Healing Dialogues and
Dialogues Consulting Group

Prelude

Cleanse ~ Restore ~ Clarify ~ Rejuvenate ~ Transform

THE 5-KEY EMOTIONAL DETOX SYSTEM

Emotional imbalance:
Journeying from clarity into deception
Occupied with uncertainty and engaged in emotional misguidedness
Innate gifts buried, life challenges revealed
Living
Blocked, Stopped, Flat-lined.

When emotionally imbalanced, we experience deeply hidden and guarded emotional disturbances. These disturbances are cleverly buried with the intention of afflicting the unconscious to cause cognizant interruptions and perplexities. They create a vacuum of emotional density with no room for clarity. These emotional imbalances are invisible and deeply colored in deception, creating pain through internal struggles long past that still control our consciousness. During these imbalances, we encounter depression, anxiety, mood changes, and unannounced behaviors. The fierce protection around these emotions enhances our emotional vulnerabilities. Any accessible stories become entwined in these vulnerabilities and need to be told.

We all have a story to tell, but in doing so we keep our most uncomfortable and painful emotions silent and hidden. When we hold these memories sacred and work diligently to avoid reliving the painful moments they contain, they become unwanted and sometimes unexpected visitors to our consciousness. Our memories of traumatic events recess in accessibility but continue to work in the darkness of our emotional vulnerabilities. Most times, these painful memories make unexpected appearances that change our characters, creating emotionally toxic moments of emotional blockage, stoppage, and flat-lining.

To recover from these emotional toxicities created by past inequities, deceptions, losses, intrusions, and traumas, we must engage in an emotional detox system. Just as we would if our bodies were infested with toxins that were causing health or weight issues, it is just as important to seek detoxing methods for emotional toxicities. In our journey toward balance of the mind, body, and spirit, we must incorporate emotional detoxification for complete, systemic, emotional balance.

Emotional detoxing is necessary to eliminate feelings that block, stop, and flat-line us from advancing and hinder our ability to flow in balance. Blocked emotions only let us reach so far, which causes a boomerang effect that rarely allows us to reach our full potential. Stopped emotions create fixations for a bondage effect that is heavy and burdensome. When emotionally stopped, we tend to function at less than 50% and lack the motivation, energy, or desire to evolve any further. When emotionally flat-lined, functioning is minimal and we keep ourselves behind an isolative barrier that hinders vital survival necessities. Here we find ourselves living in a vacuum of density, a viscosity that is difficult to penetrate or exhale. When flat-lined, we have limited ability toward self-care, physical and mental capacity, relational engagements, and survival strengths. To be blocked, stopped, or flat-lined means to function at minimal levels of emotional proficiency. Unfortunately, many times we do not recognize these emotionally toxic characteristics and compound them through substance use, self-sabotage, and victimization behaviors.

This emotional detox, which uses the "5-Key System," is your guide and journal toward eliminating those overbearing and manipulative emotional intruders and minimizing the behaviors of block, stop, and flat-line. By processing and mastering the 5-Key System, you will create your own journey into a comprehensive understanding of self. You will open doors through which you will learn to manage emotional input; promote creativity and build coping skills; develop deep cognition to experience pure forgiveness, wisdom, and healing; and transform out of feeling blocked, stopped, and flat-lined by old experiences.

To regain your innate gifts, it is important that you bridge your passions—which were handed to you from God at birth—with your mishaps, which are your past negative exposures and traumatic events that you will come to find serve a purpose. Through this system, you will begin to understand the preparation needed to enhance and strengthen your innate gifts, as well as why you endured your negative life experiences. Once you understand the necessary process of preparation and begin to bridge your passions with your mishaps, you clear the path for your own personal evolution and transformation toward emotional and systemic balance. There cannot be purpose without pain, and there cannot be transformation without understanding the pains of preparation.

Emotional balance:
Emotional prosperity in Body, Mind, and Spirit
Embraced by an abundance of peace and joy
Enhanced by internal healing and the purity of wisdom
Enveloped with forgiveness and newness of thoughts and feelings
Evolving and transforming into emotional Oneness.

found Belle a safe place to sit, not too far from the driver. When her mother left, Belle felt a sense of excitement and a little fear. She sat alone while the other passengers boarded; after a short time, a tall, beautiful young woman with blonde hair, blue eyes, and a foreign accent sat next to Belle. She was so sweet and friendly, Belle believed her to be an angel sent to protect her on her bus adventure. Belle felt safe sitting next to this woman and enjoyed gazing at her beauty.

Belle arrived in New York excited to see her father. They hugged and hugged and hugged. Immediately afterward, they went clothes shopping. Belle's father bought her a beautiful dress dotted with small delicate flowers, a new beige-colored woolen dress coat, and pretty princess shoes. Belle was very happy. They stopped to have a snack and share conversations about Belle's trip and Papa Bear's travels.

It was time for Belle to visit Papa Bear's home in Brooklyn, nestled among groups of tall brownstone apartments. Kids played in the street, and the community was full of movement. Belle recalled living in Brooklyn before her family moved to Massachusetts. She remembered playing in the streets with a little girl named Betty who always pulled Belle's two long braids. Belle gazed around with excitement, happy simply to be with her father. Having been born in the Bronx and lived in New York several years before moving, Belle loved the big city; it was in her blood.

As Belle approached the door to Papa Bear's house, a woman opened the door and smiled. This was Phyllis. Belle hoped that she was just a visiting neighbor, but soon realized that Phyllis was Papa Bear's live-in girlfriend. Belle immediately thought, "she is not pretty like my mother and she looks older than my mother." As the weekend passed, however, Belle found that Phyllis was nice to her. She even did something to Belle's hair to make it straight and pretty. She was attentive and motherly. She cooked, cleaned, and helped Belle to prepare her outfits for the next day. Belle was not used to this treatment and rather liked it.

When Belle returned home, she was excited to show her mother her new hairstyle and clothes. But her mother, who knew of Phyllis' existence, was angry that Phyllis had touched Belle's hair. Belle was confused and realized that if her mother knew about Phyllis, her parents were definitely not going to reunite as she had hoped. Belle became sad and angry.

By nine years old, Belle's contact with her father declined and her academics were suffering. She showed limited motivation to reverse this failing. Belle found herself in a blocked place. Unable to find her way through these emotions, she was without any support that could intervene. She was stuck. At first she tried to bounce back to make her father proud, but without his coming home, she could not find her way out of her trapped emotions. The more her grades worsened, the more she blamed herself and felt that she was failing her father.

Let's think about this process of "blocking." Think of it as a clogged sink, its backlog of water slowly draining and eventually drying out. This leaves a layer of residue characterized by leftover waste. Blocking is similar in the sense that we allow selectively filtered input—that is, only what we want to input—through deliberate and intentional processing. This process of only accepting our "safe" feelings leads to an eventual consumption of emotionally clouded waste—useless input that creates useless output. Still, life continues to move forward, and our input and output wane. Decision-making is difficult because we are clouded with depressive, painful feelings over which we have no control.

During the blocking process, our energy, visions, insights, joys, excitements, and other experiences shift. Most of us have at least one blockage, and our ability to cope with this blockage is determined by its magnitude and how we are able to access its root and begin to extract it. Many of us live with these blockages and experience ongoing issues of stress that can interfere with our sleep, energy, drive, relationships, weight, health, and growth.

Belle's blockage at nine years old was symptomatic of mild depression. She had built up one year of suppressed feelings, compounding them with emotional toxins, guilt, and blame. While blocked, her heart broken, she spent more and more time alone while her grades fell. She ceased to ride her red bike or dance. Belle was stuck in an internal disconnect. She was unable to make sense of her emotional input. Her time was spent crying in deep sadness.

Belle decided to fix this problem by getting her parents back together. She planned and planned and did everything she could to get their attention. Eventually, her parents realized the damage being done to Belle. Even though they were no longer together, they had remained good friends and talked frequently. They saw that Belle's interests were plummeting; she had blocked out the educational system, showed no interest in going to school, was no longer playful or energetic, and had stopped dancing. They began to understand her despair and decided to reunite. Her father left Phyllis in New York and returned home.

Papa Bear and Belle were together again. Life was in abundance. Belle immediately reignited all the projects and fun activities that she and Papa Bear once enjoyed. The relationship between Papa Bear and Belle's mother was not natural, but they tried to make it work.

When Belle was still nine years old, Papa Bear left again. This time his work took him to another country—Portugal—where he had to stay for a few years. Belle believed that she would never see her father again. She had no plan for contact; indeed no way to see Papa Bear at all. Belle's life froze. She entered a state of total disconnect and emotional stoppage.

STOPPED

By the time Belle reached ten years old, she was numb. There was a heaviness in her heart where only pain could live. She existed in a deep, pensive silence and became isolative. She still received some joy from going to Girl Scout meetings and playing with friends, but most of her days were spent in silence. She had no interest to learn and was made to repeat the fifth grade.

Let's look at the process of stopped emotions. We now have an accumulation of emotions that are impacted by blockage. Stopped emotions bring us to a hold; the clogged sink drains no longer. Now we experience an internal battle of emotions. Though we continue to function, we only do so at 50%. Our vision becomes clouded with internal pain and sadness that lack reflection. The battle between internal and external stimuli is stressful. Having to function on a daily basis through a barrier that keeps us from connecting emotionally creates a conduit for internal and physical tension, which affects our organs and compounds our emotional, mental, and physical stress. In this way, our emotional stoppage also causes stoppages in our bodily systems. Most importantly, we lose our emotional ability to move forward.

At ten years old, Belle, despite limited contact with her father, learned that he was soon to be on his way back to the United States. Belle's mother, who had been diagnosed as an epileptic, was worsening and had no family members to ask for help. An only child without aunts or uncles, Belle could only find support from her two grandmothers. She was closest to her paternal grandmother and spent a lot of time with her, especially as her mother grew less able to parent.

Grandma Venilia, whom Belle called Grandma Nina, was a good substitute for Papa Bear. Belle loved Grandma Nina's french fries and the funny-shaped donuts they would make together. Grandma Nina was a storyteller and treated Belle like a special gift just as Papa Bear used to. She allowed Belle to perform her Shirley Temple songs and dances on the kitchen table, pretending it was a stage. Belle especially enjoyed being there because it gave her someone to talk to about Papa Bear all day long. Summers with Grandma Nina meant sewing doll clothing on an old Singer pedal sewing machine, cooking fun foods, hearing stories from Cape Verde where Grandmother Nina was born, and talking about Papa Bear. Years later, Belle would still have Grandma Nina's sewing machine and her favorite recipe for *cachupa*, a Cape Verdean stew.

Every summer with Grandma Nina, Belle engaged in peer activities at the community park. She did not really know anyone there, but she enjoyed the activities. Every year, she entered the doll carriage decoration contest. One year her cousin, Leo, helped Belle decorate her doll carriage with beautifully colored tissue paper flowers. They made dozens of flowers and glued them all over the doll carriage…and she won! She would never forget sitting on the steps at City Hall and taking a picture for the local newspaper with her brightly colored, flowery carriage.

Whenever Belle visited Grandma Nina, they sang their favorite song in Krioulo, a Portuguese and African mixed dialect from Cape Verde. The name of the song was "Oh God please don't let me die before seeing my loved one." Belle replaced "loved one" with her father's name, Eduano. Belle missed her father very much. Every time she visited her grandmother's house, they sang the song over and over again. Belle always felt alive at Grandma Nina's house.

In late 1959, Belle's father returned from Portugal. Belle was still ten years old. He returned to New York and moved back in with Phyllis. For the rest of the year, Papa Bear came often to visit Belle. They enjoyed going clothes shopping, and Papa Bear often included Belle's mother in dinner plans. They got along well. These were the times Belle most looked forward to. She had to accept the fact that her father was never coming home for good, and that her parents' relationship was over.

In 1960, Papa Bear bought a house on Martha's Vineyard and decided to leave New York. Phyllis moved to Martha's Vineyard with him. Belle was happy that he would be closer to New Bedford, but sad because Phyllis was there. Belle tried to be happy with Papa Bear's move, but she wanted him to be with her mom. She could not shake the feeling of disappointment. She did not understand how her parents could get along so well, go out to dinner as a family, and spend happy times together, but still not want to live together.

These feelings created detachment and emptiness inside Belle. She did not care that she had to repeat the fifth grade. She refused to go to school or do her homework, and would not meet with her teachers. When she did go to school, she remained mentally and emotionally absent. In three years, Belle's grades drop from A's to F's. She could not pull it together. The more she heard her father's voice in her head telling her how important education was, the more guilt and shame she felt. The voice was strong enough, however, that she knew she had to at least pass to the sixth grade.

Belle's internal emptiness left her numb. Every day she skipped school (which was often), she sat in her mother's pink-and-green flowered armchair by the bedroom window. Most days, Belle sat and watched as children walked into her school building. On days when her mother worked, Belle stayed home all day. When the school day ended, Belle returned to her position at the window to watch the other children leave school.

Belle felt like a failure and was deeply saddened that she disappointed her family, especially her father. She knew she must return to school, but she was so far behind that even when she did attend, she sat in her classroom chair in a fog. Belle had no motivators, no supporters, and no one to encourage her. She started to give up and ceased to care. Her father's voice continued to stress the importance of doing well in school, but she could not find the strength to improve. By the grace of God she finally passed the fifth grade, and the relief she felt at finally being able to tell her father about her progress helped her to complete middle school, but barely.

During the summer of 1960, Belle established a close relationship with a 16-year-old Portuguese girl named Marie. Marie was a pretty girl who always wore a long ponytail and looked like she belonged in the 1950s play "Grease." She was tomboyish, loved music, and was quite advanced for her age. Marie was married to an older Cape Verdean man, and they lived on the third floor of her parent's home. Marie, six years older than Belle, was attentive and loyal to her. She changed Belle's perception on life and filled the need left by her absentee parents. Belle felt nurtured and supported again. She finally had someone she could embrace, talk to, and trust. Marie showed true fondness for Belle.

Marie, being young and rebellious, became Belle's hero. Belle's eleven years had been full of guilt, shame, and blame, locked up with blocked, stopped, and flat-lined emotions. Belle hungered to be around Marie every day, all the time. Marie gave Belle a sense of maturity. She introduced Belle to cigarettes, allowed her to hang out in her apartment, and taught her life lessons. Although a rebel herself, Marie did not allow Belle to go beyond smoking and hanging out.

Belle's mother, learning of what happened during their time together, attempted to stop the relationship between Belle and Marie. Belle did not obey, continuing to be with Marie. Unable to control Belle, her mother sent her back to her Grandma Nina's house. Belle was angry and resentful and experienced an internal crash that culminated in an emotional flat-line.

Flat-Lined

When we flat-line, we lose consciousness of what is important: our values and morals, our family attachments and sources of love, our innate gifts and passions. Life becomes a dark, dense, and dispelling place that holds no emotion. A flat-line state is a major disconnection from life associated with varying forms of depression. It is an unresponsiveness that is like an emotional death. It is difficult to take a deep breath or find empathy; it is a lethargic state of mind.

At twelve years old, Belle was in the seventh grade but skipped school at every chance she could. She had completely blocked all memories of middle school. She finished the seventh grade but had no memory as to how it happened. She was living a flat-lined existence.

Belle's mother became concerned with Belle's deep depressive behaviors. She decided that Belle would spend the whole summer with her father on Martha's Vineyard. Belle was happy to be with her father, but she was not ready to leave Marie, who had been considering a move to California with her newborn baby girl, Lisa. Belle loved Marie and Lisa so much that she had created in her mind that they were her family. She trusted that Marie would never leave her. Ultimately, Marie convinced Belle that being with her father was the best decision Belle could make.

Belle and her mother went out shopping for summer clothes. Belle's mother always bought her daughter quality clothing and had Belle's hair done weekly. They bought bright orange, baby blue, and sea green "pedal pusher" pants with matching tops and new boat sneakers. Belle was very excited for the summer, but still unsure about leaving Marie and Lisa.

Belle arrived at Martha's Vineyard and was happy to be with her father until she realized that Phyllis was less than pleased with her presence there. Immediately, Belle knew that this would be the end of her happy times with Papa Bear. Still, she was so happy in the moment that she felt ready to adjust to anything. It helped that the house was beautiful. Belle thought, *"Wow! A real home with a real, structured family lifestyle."*

Belle decided to get Phyllis to like her. With her mother so ill and unable to parent her, Belle was ready to accept Phyllis as a mother substitute. She craved the motherly attentions that Phyllis gave her in New York. However, after Belle's mother reacted in anger to Phyllis' having touched Belle's hair, Phyllis changed towards Belle. This did not stop Belle from trying to win Phyllis over.

Much of Belle's life at home had been caring for her mother and protecting her from seizures. Belle's bedroom was next to her mother's, and every night she listened for the swallowing and clapping noises that preceded the seizures. Young as she was, Belle had learned how to prevent the seizures from coming. She always had a bowl of water, a face cloth, and an object to press down on her mother's tongue at the ready. If she could not stop the seizure, she could at least stop her mother from injuring herself.

Summer ended on fairly positive note, and plans were made for Belle to return the following summer. Belle prepared to enter the eighth grade feeling more accomplished and less emotionally challenged. The thought of having easy access to her father was helpful and encouraging. However, her mother was unable to work due to her seizures, and they began to experience financial hardship. Belle and her mother moved from their home into a housing project. This crushed Belle's ego and meant that she had to move away from Marie and the lifestyle she knew.

After the move, Belle began acting out. She hung out with kids who did not make good choices, joined secret peer "clubs," and experimented with marijuana and alcohol. She was caught shoplifting and had to see a probation officer. Belle managed to keep this from her father, but her mother, unable to manage her, sent Belle to her grandmother's house. Once again, Belle found herself removed from friends and the culture she was growing into.

Grandma Nina lived in a predominately white community, unlike the diverse one where Belle came from. At this point, Belle had no option but to stay with her grandmother. The only highlight was that she now had more access to her father. This helped Belle to feel less emotionally imbalanced, but she continued to feel blocked, stopped, and disconnected. She walked to school every day with her male cousin, Stevie. She felt good about being with her cousin, but retained no memory of school. She functioned in numbness, barely achieving the D's required for her to enter high school.

Belle's mother allowed her to come back to the community for visits. During one such visit, Belle was caught drunk by Marie, who took her back to her mother's house. Belle's behavior worsened; she drank, hung out with guys, smoked cigarettes, and occasionally dabbled in marijuana (though she disliked drugs or substances that she felt controlled her). Belle's mother was done; all she could do was call Belle's father. He came to talk to Belle. Her mother informed him of everything that had been going on with Belle. For the first time in Belle's life, she experienced her father's anger; he was so angry that with a closed fist he hit the kitchen table top. Her father had never lost his cool before. They decided that he would to talk to Phyllis about Belle living with them through high school.

Belle knew this would never happen. Her previous summer visit made her feel like Cinderella (Phyllis had two older daughters). Thoughts of living permanently with her father on Martha's Vineyard were exciting, but she knew that life under Phyllis' control would be an imprisonment. In passive ways, Phyllis reminded Belle that she and her mother were not groomed well enough for her. Phyllis spent time "grooming" Belle so to not embarrass her. Belle recalled past visits to her father when she was allowed to play quietly on the front porch, creating games with the ants industriously building their homes. She could watch those ants for hours, trying to figure out their patterns.

Phyllis' grandchildren come to visit, giving Belle someone to play with. Belle quickly learned that they were to be role models for her, as she was not allowed to have her own friends come over, attend the many activities for girls offered on the Island, or go to the beaches. Belle's only real outlet was an understanding, loving girl named Maggie who lived down the road. Maggie spent hours with Belle, trying to understand her emotional demise. It was because of Maggie and her family that Belle survived the summer and found hope in living. Later, two other women would intervene and embrace Belle; her best friend Reb's mother and her next-door neighbor who employed Belle as a babysitter.

Needless to say, the course laid out by Phyllis was not what Belle had bargained for. Still, she would do anything to be with her father. Things had changed, however, as her father could show his nurturing feelings toward Belle around Phyllis. Belle fell from feeling stopped directly into feeling emotionally flat-lined. When around Phyllis, she had to contain her emotions and learned not to reveal how she felt to her father.

Belle was fourteen years old when Papa Bear talked to Phyllis about Belle moving in with them to attend high school. This came as a shock to Phyllis, and she spent the summer being abusive toward Belle and becoming increasingly avoidant, distant, and less interactive with her. Toward the end of the summer, Belle's father told Phyllis that Belle would indeed be coming to live with them.

Phyllis gave him an ultimatum: either her or Belle. He chose Belle, and Phyllis left.

Imagine at fourteen having already faced depression, loss, abuse, detachment, limited or selective nurturing, and emotional flat-lining. These emotional battles live inside each of us, and many children are exposed daily to their challenges. Many of these emotional trials are traumatic in nature, or can be the result of genetic predisposition or environmental, cultural, or social conditions. When we are infected by this "emotional bacteria" of sorts, which can be pathological, our infections can be indefinite. The appropriate prescriptions, plans, supports, and interventions are necessary immediately. For many, the infection festers and creates a life of victimization and, in some instances, psychosis.

In Belle's case, the victimization was just at its beginning stages at age fourteen. Her unresolved internal triggers would only intensify, and the block, stop and flat-line indicators would become her coping mechanisms and way of life.

So let's recap. First there is life, which sometimes comes with challenges. As we move through life's developmental stages, we evolve at our own pace. As we become more aware, we become acclimated to the environment to which we are exposed. Eventually, what we are exposed to will form our character. During this process, we can experience positive growth or negative decline, and develop our ability to escape and manage this decline—the block, stop, and flat-line. We all have a story to tell, and it is best we tell it honestly.

In this guide, you will be introduced to a "5 Key System" for emotional detoxing. This system is an internal management mechanism for controlling the emotional indicators of block, stop and flat-line. Detoxing is a familiar concept to us, and emotional detoxing is an important step on our journey to "Oneness." Dr. Celina has created the idea of a "Symphony in the Key of Oneness." This symphony depends on our emotional detoxification through the 5-Key System, where we cleanse the suppressed, restore balance, find clarity, experience internal rejuvenation, and transform. This leaves us free to follow our passions and internal gifts that once were blocked, stopped, or flat-lined. The 5-Key System: Cleanse, Restore, Clarify, Rejuvenate, and Transform, is the thread by which we can align to this journey. At the end of your journey, be prepared to receive the innate gifts you were born with and experience the wisdom and joy that follow.

1st Key
CLEANSE

Chapter 2

KEY #1
EMOTIONAL CLEANSING

There are moments in our lives when we experience negative emotional surges that cause blockage, stoppage, or flat-lining. In these moments, we have the choice to dismiss, repress, and attempt to forgot them; or address, work through, and release them. Our stories can be difficult to tell with honesty, especially when this requires reliving a painful event. What we often fail to understand is that when we repress these emotions and bury our secrets, they continue to live within us and create a level of toxicity that is emotionally and physically crippling. This makes the need for emotional detoxing, or the removal of the multiplex of emotional intruders, intrinsically important.

Let's look at the statistics. According to the National Institute of Mental Health (NIMH)'s 2014 research, 9.8 million adults over the age of 18 have been diagnosed with severe mental health issues in the United States, which is 4.2% or approximately 1 in 25 adults. Predominate in these statistics are Caucasian females 26 to 49 years of age at 5.0%. Least predominate are Asian males 50 years and older at 2.4%. The rate of those with any type of mental health issue is 43.6 million adults aged 18 years or older, which is 18% of the U.S. population. Again, most predominate are Caucasian females 26 to 49 years of age (21.8%), and least predominate are Asian males 50 years of age and older (14.1%). According to more recent research, approximately 1 in 5 adults in the U.S. experience mental health issues annually; this is 43.5 million or 18.5% of the adult population. For youth ages 13 to 18, it is estimated that 21.4% experience severe mental health issues, and 13% children ages 8 to 15 suffer from mental health issues. NIMH statistics estimate that severe mental illness costs the U.S. $193.5 billion in lost earnings every year.

Overall, 1 in 5 adults in the U.S. suffer with some type of mental illness. In many cases, emotional complications are associated with these mental health issues. This combination of issues impacts our behaviors, feelings, and responses. If we compound the emotional and mental health issues with physiological and health complaints, we then magnify the problem. When these complications begin to intensify and interweave, they create a block, stop and flat-lining effect. NIMH research confirms that people experiencing severe mental health issues have an increase in chronic medical conditions. This gives us multiple layers of intertwined emotional toxicity, creating a vice grip around our organs and blocking, stopping, or flat-lining our very existence. NIMH studies also indicate that suicide is the tenth leading cause of death in the U.S. and the third leading cause of death for those aged 15 to 24 years. This only intensifies the need for emotional cleaning as a means to rejuvenate life and create a meaningful existence.

When emotional battles combine with organ dysfunction, they create an internal disharmony and imbalance in our overall system. If we incorporate the daily toxicity and stressful interactions that compound the already internalized emotional contaminants with socioeconomic stresses, academic and employment challenges, community violence, accidental deaths, cognitive and neurological conditions, natural physiological developments, and existing health issues, we have a dangerous accumulation of substantial internal toxicity.

Let's take a look at how emotions can affect our organs. Research indicates that emotional volatilities have physical consequences in the form of major complications. Stress is a major variable that affects our health in many ways. Negative stressors are the catalyst for many physical illnesses, but they also provide us with the strength to cope with life's circumstances. However, stresses that are not surmountable tend to have negative impacts in the body, mind, and spirit. The following are examples of how emotional impact can render our organs vulnerable.

The Emotional Life of Our Organs

HEART: The heart, as a primary organ, it is very sensitive to emotionality. Explosive emotions like hostility, anger, extreme irritability, and internal torment clearly affect the heart. Emotions that are less visible, such as loneliness, withdrawal, isolation, grief, and depression, also have an effect on the heart.

LUNGS: The lungs work with the heart and are just as vulnerable to many of the same emotional conditions. Intense emotional material can create constriction in the lungs, leading to respiratory conditions. Major grief, loss, and bereavement are catalysts for chronic respiratory diseases.

THROAT: It has been notated that the throat is affected by not speaking the truth. In extreme cases, one can become muted. Feeling a "lump in your throat" can be caused by intense sentimentality.

STOMACH: Harboring intense emotions like rage, torment, and hate can lead to several stomach conditions. These conditions (e.g., ulcers, gastritis) coupled with melancholic emotional tensions (e.g., anxiety, pensiveness, depression) can lead to difficulties with anorexia and other appetite disorders.

SPLEEN: When the spleen is affected by melancholic emotions, the natural flow through the digestive system is distressed, causing an agitation that leads to gas, bloating, and other such irritations in the abdominal area.

INTESTINES AND BOWELS: The intestines are often affected by psychosomatic expression or emotions that disturb the upper digestive system (e.g., the liver, gall bladder, stomach, and spleen). When impacted by melancholic emotions, the middle and lower intestinal tracts can experience an obstruction in flow and function.

COLON: Excessive melancholic emotion (e.g., profound feelings of worry, anxiety, nervousness, stress, emotional insecurities) affect the natural functioning of the colon. These emotional disturbances can be the culprits behind constipation, irritable bowel syndrome, and even colitis.

KIDNEYS: Intense experiences of fear and shock can cause extreme damage to the kidneys. These heightened emotions can cause one to lose of control of their kidneys and bladder function, resulting in spontaneous urination.

ADRENAL GLANDS: The adrenal glands are affected by excessive stress. The fight-or-flight adrenaline response is triggered by a severe form of stress and emotional explosiveness. When stresses are excessive or chronic, they can lead to weight gain and elevated blood sugar levels.

MALE REPRODUCTIVE ORGANS: Male impotence or sexual dysfunction usually due to a physical complaint can also be due to emotional tensions presented through fear, performance anxiety, insecurity, or fear of inadequacy.

FEMALE REPRODUCTIVE ORGANS: Female frigidity occurs when trust has been violated, which provokes feelings of anxiety and a shutting down of emotional capacity.

Alignment of Emotions with Bodily Systems

JOY is obtainable when there is a deep connection to selflessness and an internal cleansing that creates a strong spiritual bond. The inability to reach these depths or to experience overwhelming joy can initiate anxiety and heart palpitations. Joy affects the heart and small intestines.

ANGER is an intense emotional response to feelings of agitation, resentment, rage, or the strong response to a **negatively** perceived situation. This response creates an internal disturbance that initiates a loss of energy, high blood pressure and respiratory issues, headaches, and dizziness. Anger affects the liver and gall bladder.

ANXIETY is a state of inner turmoil associated with excessive worry, fear, and a generalized disposition of overwhelming visual, sensory, and emotional perception. These presentations can cause shortness of breath, heart palpitations, fight-or-flight responses, ulcers, and other complications that affect the stomach, spleen, large intestine, and lungs.

GRIEF is an inward emotion that expresses a crippling internal sadness. Mourning, the outward expression of grief, can cause difficulties in the lungs and respiratory system and inhibit energy from circulating through the body. Grief affects the lungs and large intestines.

PENSIVENESS is an emotion characterized by excessive thinking and melancholia. The deep retreat into thought, coupled with intense sadness or depressive feelings, impact the spleen and manifest in lethargy. The stomach is also affected with bouts of gas, distension, and bloating.

FEAR is the emotional response to danger. Fear is an internal alert for self-protection. Fear effects the kidneys and bladder and causes involuntary urination.

FRIGHT is the sudden intense perception of an unexpected threat. Fright has an immediate effect on the heart, and can also affect the kidneys and bladder.

The idea of emotions and stress affecting our organs is not a new phenomenon. Consider the effects of chronic mental health and medical conditions and the long-term effects of these two dynamics. It is conceivable that cleansing our emotions can only benefit the associated organs and create an internal balance to promote healthier results. It is clear that addressing your negative emotional content will increase your clarity, movability, creativity, functionality, and energy. With the right emotional cleansing ingredients, you can enjoy a beautifully crafted internal symphony.

An ongoing concern is that many of these challenges begin in childhood, even at birth. NIMH research estimates that mental health illness affects 13 to 20% (1 in 5) of children in the United States. The impacts on these children can be devastating. Mental health conditions can potentially intensify through developmental and cognitive issues, familial and genetic complications, academic and social pressures, peer and sibling rivalry, and other traumatic experiences. Some of these complications are compounded and difficult to identify, becoming multifaceted over time.

Belle's Journey toward Cleansing

Belle's complexities began at eight years old when she started showing signs of dysthymia (also known as persistent depressive disorder), which is similar in characteristics to depression but less severe. For adults, a dysthymic diagnosis is valid when the patient experiences a depressed mood on most days for at least a two-year period; children or adolescents can be diagnosed from an irritable mood lasting at least one year. According to the DSM V, the criteria for diagnosis is the presence of at least two of the following symptoms: overeating or lack of appetite, sleeping too much or having difficulty sleeping, fatigue or lack of energy, poor self-esteem, difficulty concentrating or making decisions, and feeling of hopelessness.

Belle's emotional instabilities early in her life clearly met the criteria for a diagnosis of dysthymia disorder. During her flat-lining episodes, Belle bordered on receiving a diagnosis for major depression. Belle shifted from being a happy, innocent girl who loved riding her red bike, dancing in her soft white shoes, and being her father's fishing side-kick to a child controlled by pain and sadness. Her parents' separation caused an internal crash where her emotions became misplaced, locked, and shut-down. This put Belle into a cycle of endless grief.

To protect herself from her emotions, Belle learned to cope by avoiding, withdrawing, and isolating herself from all facets of emotional content, both positive and negative. Further compounding these emotions was the fact that her mother, Rose, was chronically ill and required Belle's care. Rosie, as everyone called her, was as beautiful as Lena Horne and an impressive dancer who loved to sing, but was laden with epilepsy, depression, and severe anxiety. Although she loved Belle and kept her safe, she was unable to parent her due to her handicapping conditions.

By middle school, Belle's emotional burdens were affecting her health. She lost a lot of weight, had an extended stomach, and appeared malnourished. Her distaste for school grew as school children bullied her for being so skinny. Her peers threatened her physically and called her names. A bullying chant was created using Belle's first and last names, which translated into "Chicken Shit." There was no support system for Belle at school, so she would often run home crying, feeling useless. Because Belle rarely went to school, she did not make any friends or develop a peer support system. Most kids and school staff did not know her.

By the time Belle was fourteen, she had experienced her parents' divorce, been made to repeat the fifth grade, had limited adult nurturing, dealt with her father's new relationship, experienced discord from her father's girlfriend, been bullied, put on probation for stealing, had her first cigarette and taste of alcohol, attended very little school, and had a taste of poverty. On one occasion, Belle was so hungry due to poverty that her downstairs neighbor offered her some homemade rice pudding. Belle was excited because she loved rice pudding but her mother never cooked and there was rarely any food in the house. Belle usually had to eat at her maternal grandmother's house. On this day, she ran downstairs to get the rice pudding and when she had it in her hands, it slipped and fell onto the stairs. Belle was so hungry that she ate the rice pudding off the dirty steps. After that experience, Belle never ate rice pudding again.

Belle's maternal grandmother, Henriquetta, or better known as Katy, did all the food shopping, cooking, and cleaning for Belle's home. Fearing that Belle's mother would be injured or die during an epileptic episode, she did everything for them. Grandma Katy was a caring yet rigid woman, a functional caretaker with a heart for helping others. She was not very loving, but deeply caring and with a funny sense of humor. Grandma Katy and Belle's mother were both in agreement to send Belle to her father's to attend high school. Grandma Katy feared that Belle's behaviors would cause her mother more harm than good.

At fifteen, Belle entered high school. When she reflected on her past, she feared for her high school future. She was sure she would fail and be in even more trouble. However, when Belle went to live with her father on Martha's Vineyard, Phyllis left for nine months (after Belle's father chose his daughter in the presented ultimatum). These nine months were the happiest of Belle's life. She and Papa Bear created their own world filled with fishing, boating, ice cream, table pool, music, swimming, long conversations, laugher, playing guitar, and helping her father maintain his business correspondence and records.

At some point, Belle had an epiphany that made her stop in her tracks and cry for the first time in a long time. She realized that her father chose her over Phyllis. She now believed that her father knew that Phyllis had disrupted their family and that he would not allow her to do it again. Belle saw that her father saw her about to get lost in a destructive world, and that he recognized that only he could save her. Belle was so relieved, she felt an emotional connection to parental love and acceptance for the first time in seven years.

For nine months, Belle excelled. She saw her mother frequently on weekends and had her father's love and nurturance every day. She felt clarity for the first time and went through emotional cleansing. Every night, she slept with the reassurance that her father had chosen her over Phyllis. She smiled, thanked God, and slept well. She knew that nothing would ever come between them again, and swore to do everything the right way to make her father proud. While she still faced some academic challenges, her grades climbed from D's to C's. She re-involved herself in school clubs and stopped skipping class. She was even rewarded every year for perfect school attendance. Belle learned how to balance her relationships with her mother and father, finally feeling joy and peace.

Nine months later, Phyllis returned promising change—but she did not change. Belle stayed in school on the Vineyard, but found herself visiting her mother more often. Her relationship with her father remained strong, but as expected their time together lessened. Phyllis' return signaled Belle's shift back into misery.

Belle associated her deepest pain with the time spent on Martha's Vineyard with Phyllis. This pain formed over years of emotional abuse. The most difficult torment she experienced was watching the hateful, despicable, and wicked ways in which Phyllis treated Belle's father, whom she saw as the nicest and most generous man on earth. Phyllis never worked, but traveled around the world and lived like a queen. Phyllis' biggest contention was Belle's father's love for his daughter; Phyllis knew that being his only child, Belle would eventually become the recipient of his fortune. Twelve years older than Belle's parents, Phyllis was anxious to keep her new husband's financial success out of the hands of Belle and her mother.

Phyllis had two daughters about the age of Belle's mother. One daughter had three children, whose company Belle enjoyed. The oldest, a girl, was a lot of fun and loved to dance like Belle. She was kind and treated Belle with love. The two boys were just as much fun and showed an interest in including Belle in their family. Phyllis' other daughter never had children. Belle became very close to this daughter, who was youthful and loved to party. Whenever Belle visited her, she was treated as a guest from New York; she showed the daughter and her husband the latest dances from the city. Belle enjoyed this task, though her shyness kept her from dancing fully; still, she gave the friendly couple just enough for them to want more.

Sadly, no one and nothing could save Belle from Phyllis' wrath. Phyllis refused to provide Belle any compliments, constructive criticism, support, help with homework, enjoyable activities, phone calls from friends, or friend visits. She allowed her to listen to R&B music only in the basement, set her a list of daily chores, and did not involve her in family conversations or activities. When Belle was allowed to participate, such as on family fishing trips, she had to keep firm boundaries. She could not show too much happiness or excitement. Most of Belle's weekends and summers were spent cleaning and re-cleaning every inch of the house down to the last small-paned window. Belle's hatred for those windows would persist long into her future.

Belle has gone from Shirley Temple to Cinderella. She waited for her fairy godmother to come and take Phyllis back to New York on a flying coach. Belle survived her years on Martha's Vineyard by having secret getaways with her father. Without Phyllis knowing, the pair went for ice cream many nights (despite Papa Bear's diabetes) in an effort to help Belle gain weight. They snuck away to go swimming in the lake, dig for clams, and fish. They frequently visited the beach simply to lie in the sand, talking or playing with the dog. Belle's best memory was the day Papa Bear put her into an inner tube and swam under the water, pulling Belle by her feet to the shallow sand bar to dig for clams and chase scallops. These moments held Belle together and gave her hope. Her special time with Papa Bear became Belle's glue.

Most of Belle's days were spent in the house around Phyllis, trying to say the right words so as to not make every conversation into a "teaching moment." When Belle's father was not around, Belle stayed quietly in her room or in the basement to avoid conflict or the next put-down by Phyllis. Belle was never disrespectful to Phyllis, nor did she bother her father with complaining. She accepted the good with the bad and chose her battles carefully. Being with her father far outweighed Phyllis' emotional abuse. Belle soon learned how to balance these daily interactions and found the quality of the time with her father to be more valuable than the quantity of time spent on Martha's Vineyard.

In April 1965 when she was sixteen, Belle was raped and her virginity taken. Having always wanted to save her virginity for marriage, this devastated her. Belle had never even kissed a boy, not because she did not want to, but because she was so skinny that no boys were interested in talking to her. She had never considered being intimate with a boy, and intercourse was out of the question. The only other contact she ever had with a male was with Phyllis' son-in-law, who made soft sexual advances toward her but left her alone after she ignored him.

Belle had to live with the secret of her rape, telling only her best friend, Reb. When she was seventeen, the same son-in-law made a more aggressive sexual advance toward Belle and molested her in her bedroom while the adults were in the living room playing Bridge. Entering Belle's dark room, the man approached her bed and whispered her name. Belle recognized the danger but felt trapped, afraid that Phyllis would blame her for whatever was to happen. The son-in-law quickly molested her and planned for another time. Belle was frightened but told no one, trying instead to keep away from him and moving to an upstairs bedroom. During this time, Phyllis set a strange mission to convince Belle's father that Belle was a whore who had been sleeping with fishermen since a young age. One afternoon, Belle's father told her that, tired of hearing Phyllis' foolish accusations, he wanted to go to the family doctor to prove Belle's virginity.

At this news, Belle suffered an anxiety attack. What could she do? The tests would disgrace her father and prove Phyllis right, even though she was very wrong; this would tear her father apart and ruin his trust in Belle. Fearing being left alone again, Belle became a wreck. She went to her best friend for advice, thinking that if she explained the situation to her family doctor and paid him not to tell the truth, perhaps the problem would go away. Reb told her that would never work because the island was too small and the doctor would never take Belle's side.

Belle went into panic mode. She called another friend, Paula, who lived near her mother. She told her the circumstances and formed a new plan: find someone to marry her at eighteen, despite her never having had a boyfriend or ever being an object of interest. Paula told Belle she could introduce her to someone.

Belle succeeded in delaying the doctor's appointment. One week later, the boy recommended by Paula (really a man of twenty-three years), Richard, came to visit. Belle worked some magic, and Richard agreed to marry her in one month's time. Belle convinced Richard to meet with her father that day to tell him of their intentions to marry. Richard knew he was getting a good deal because Belle's father lived a visibly comfortable lifestyle. He saw dollars instead of Belle, but Belle didn't care. This was the saddest day in Papa Bear's life, and the happiest in Phyllis'. Upon informing her father and Phyllis of the marital plans, Belle was told by Phyllis, "Once you're out of here, you don't return."

Belle didn't really care, as her only intent was to save her father from shame. One month later, Belle dropped out of high school in her senior year so her father could walk her down the aisle to a stranger. In their married life, Richard beat Belle on a daily basis, keeping her locked in the house without allowance for visitors. This lasted three years, only because Belle had nowhere to go. For the first year, Belle and Richard live in Newport on Rhode Island. During this year, Belle's father worried about Belle and looked for a way to bring her back home to Martha's Vineyard. He asked Richard to move to the island to work for him. He also offered to pay their rent and buy them a car. Richard agreed and Belle felt rescued by her father yet again. Belle knew that this was her escape from being beaten and raped almost daily. She envisioned returning to school to finish her last year and graduate high school.

About a year and a half into living on Martha's Vineyard, Richard, who in the past beat his own father, decided to teach Belle's father a lesson. He told Belle that he intended to beat her father for no reason. Seeking a way to protect her father from this severely violent man, Belle created a getaway plan to escape from Richard and save her father from her husband's violent rage. Belle decided that her only way out was to tell her father the truth about Richard's abusiveness and his plan to hurt, though she would not divulge why she married him in the first place.

To add further stress, Grandma Nina had a stroke and moved in with Richard and Belle. If Belle was to escape her husband, she had to first make plans for Grandma Nina's care. Phyllis refused to help Belle's father with the care of his mother, so Belle and Papa Bear arranged for care in Grandma Nina's home off the island. Once Grandma Nina was settled, Belle's father decided once again to rescue Belle against Phyllis' wishes. He placed Belle in the cottage next to his house with the promise that she would return to school and finish her last year. Belle could finally take a deep breath and relax, though Phyllis was fuming. Belle's father reported Richard to the local police, forcing him to leave the island.

At twenty-one, Belle finished her last year of high school but could not escape the secret life of a victim. After her graduation, Belle moved to Boston to live with Reb. She never was able to consider college before, but her father always believed that Belle was capable of obtaining a college degree. Belle worked several jobs and eventually moved into her own apartment, which she later shared with Paula.

At this stage in Belle's life, she had not gone through successful emotional cleansing. Belle was still tarnished by negative past experiences. She did not know who she is nor what she was capable of doing. She lived in a stricken world tied down by doubt and disappointments. Belle had no understanding of the world she was about to encounter, so she entered it without preparation or certainty, still suffering from a disconnected ego and emotional disengagement.

At twenty-seven, Belle had her first serious relationship with a man named Al, who reminded her of her father. He was protective of Belle and encouraging, an angel sent to help her move along a life path she didn't even know existed. Al provided a normalcy to which Belle had never been exposed. Belle's father liked Al, as they shared much in common. Belle's father was especially happy with Al because he treated Belle well. Al convinced Belle to attend a two-year college program. Belle thought him crazy, but he was so supportive that they attended together. Belle decided to major in accounting because she once enjoyed helping her father with his books. She received her first A since the second grade. This initiated Belle's academic career, which she did not stop until she achieved her doctorate. Still, even these achievements did not stop her secret life as a victim.

Imagine the most formative years of your life dominated by continued disturbances, inconsistencies, tragedies, and inner turmoil like Belle's. Feeling lost within yourself without a GPS, you have no way out of the depths; you are locked down and away, flat-lined and breathless. The daily stress of living with these emotional intruders while trying to balance life, especially at a young age, is devastating. So, how do you cope with this imbalance? At a young age, the only alternatives are negative interactions, and coping mechanisms are limited to self-mutilation, substance abuse, negative transformations, anger, sadness, depression, anxiety, seeking love through sex, and other behaviors damaging to emotional and mental health. Like Belle, having to walk in the shadow of darkness without a shepherd leads you into a maze of perplexity and harbored negativity. Luckily, it is possible to clear out these infestations of thought through the 5-Key System and open the door to healing and emotional freedom.

The Journey to Emotional Cleansing

Let's begin the journey. Remember the full instructions for Key 1 Cleanse, is in the corresponding workbook. Please read the entire workbook before proceeding with the emotional detox. We will take hold of Key #1 and begin a system of cleansing into Oneness.

You will begin this journey with the journaling prompts provided below. Please be sure to read the instructions for journaling in the attached workbook before beginning the cleansing process.

Journaling Prompts for Emotional Cleansing

I. Key To Exposing Emotional Stories and writing your "Global Emotional Biography"

On the blank list available in the provided journal workbook, do the following:

- Create an emotional memory list.
- Order the list from the least difficult to the most difficult emotional memory.
- If your memory has any level of emotional impact that blocks, stops, or flat-lines, it is an emotion in need of cleansing.

II. Key to addressing emotional intruders

On the Emotional Impact page in the provided journal, summarize your stories. From your emotional memory list, find the main issue in each story (e.g., divorce). Once this is complete, list the impact of these issues, emotions, and situations as follows:

- Column A: List your main issues (*e.g., divorce*).
- Column B: Rank the impacts of the issue according to intensity (*0 = least difficult; 10 = most difficult*).
- Column C: List the emotions associated with your identified issues (*e.g., sadness, anger, blame, fear, shame, depression, grief*).
- Column D: Describe the conditions and person(s) involved (*e.g., parents, occurred at age eight*).

III. Key to oneness through journaling

Read the workbook instructions before proceeding with the following steps.

- Identify your support system clearly.
- Create your own affirmation or use an affirmation provided.
- Feel and visualize your affirmation.
- Begin with your easiest memory or story. You can create your own storybook, be it written, videotaped, or audio. However you chose to document you story, try to make the memory as vivid as possible. Be sure to keep your memories in a safe place. In documenting these stories, make sure as well to keep yourself safe. Attempt to access as much memory as possible. If it becomes difficult, stop and reach out to your support system.
- Create your first internal video. Summarize the video material in the area provided. As many times as necessary, rerun the video until you feel you have completed your memory of the event. Don't forget to use your internal remote to stop, rewind, pause, and fast forward.
- While you are creating the stream of memories through your internal video, additional memories may emerge. Use the "Note" section of the daily journal page to jot down these emerging memories. At the end of this journey, merge the new information into the story that you created previously.

- Using the Emotional Content Scale, measure your level of impact following each internal videoing session. Remember that you are trying to achieve a level of "3" or lower. Always do a body scan to find where you experience discomfort. If your emotional impact is a 3 or lower and your body scan reveals no discomfort, your cleanse has been successful.
- In the Sensitization area of the journal, document where in your body there continues to be discomfort or comfort.
- The Release section of the journal is the final cleansing step. Here you will document each release, how it occurred, how you feel about the memory now, what your coping mechanism is for similar events, how your supports helped in the process, and what part of the process enabled you to release the memory or story.

Remember, a single memory or story may take many times to reach a full cleanse. Each time you revisit the memory, an emotional cleanse is underway. The mere fact that you have opened that cubical again and are taking control over the experience allows for more cleansing. This is empowering and will bring your shuttered memories into consciousness. It is in this consciousness that you will eradicate emotional intruders. Beginning with the least difficult memory will allow you to learn your process, build coping strategies to deal with the intruders, and help control your anxiety related to visualizing the memory. This will give you the confidence, emotional tools, and techniques necessary to approach your more difficult memories. Your journey to Oneness is just beginning. Your goal in Oneness is to create your own symphony, one key at a time.

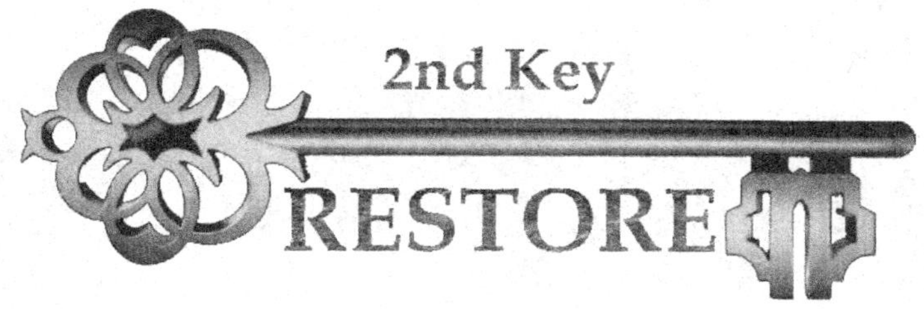
2nd Key
RESTORE

Chapter 3

KEY #2
RESTORATION AND HEALING

When we think of the emotional healing process, we think about the discomfort of having to revisit painful and sometimes horrific memories. Most times, these memories are too difficult to revisit and too painful to process. We tend to peek into the room where we've hidden our darkest recollections, close the door quickly, lock it, then double lock it. We rebury these secrets, but this only allows them to continue to torment and consume us.

As these painful memories take residence in their secure holding cells, they actively dominate and manipulate us emotionally. These emotions shadow our every existence and, without invitation, participate in all that we do. These memories have an almost supernatural power to redirect our thoughts, attitudes, and behaviors without our notice. We have to wonder why we protect and keep these menacing memories. These thought predators permeate the depths of our interiors and block, stop, and flat-line our emotional advancement. Yet, we continue to insulate and protect them. There are no borders or boundaries these intruders will not cross. No one is immune from them, regardless of religious belief, education, and financial stature.

So, why do we protect these memories, and why are we afraid to expose them? Over the past thirty years, I have had the opportunity to meet and speak with a diverse group of individuals. Many of these individuals were aware of an emotional imbalance, but unaware of how past history affected it. Many were unable to revisit the potential precipitants that gave birth to these emotional blockages, stoppages, and flat-lining behaviors. The more traumatic the events, the less able individuals were to revisit their repressed feelings and images. However, when these same people felt safe and had appropriate support systems in place, clinical interventions were effective. These individuals found the internal strengths and knowledge to evacuate their emotional intruders. They arrived at a place where they were emotionally ready to move forward and not be held at bay by painful memories that had already occupied too much of their lifetimes. Once they moved forward and freed themselves of these intruders, they were able to find purpose through "the trail of pain into the path of success and transformation."

Belle's Journey through Restoration

It was 1973, and Belle's father was sending her to San Francisco to rekindle her relationship with Marie. Belle was extremely excited. She has not seen Marie for more than twelve years, so it was bound to be a sweet reunion. Paula, Belle's best friend and travel partner, shared in this happy experience. It was a week of reminiscing, bonding, and catching up. Marie, now twenty-nine years old, continued in her role as mother to Belle. The greatest moment was when Belle saw Marie's daughter, Lisa, who was just a newborn when they left for California. Lisa looked like an angel, and Belle felt a warm tenderness toward her. The visit had a resolving and healing power.

Marie took Belle and Paula sightseeing to fun spots in the city. At night they went club hopping, and Belle became known as the Dancing Belle of San Francisco. At one club, she meets her very first *real* crush. He was tall, handsome, educated (attending Berkeley Law School, Boalt Hall), well dressed, and so much fun. Belle was consumed. They stayed in contact for the remainder of the weekend, and he seemed very interested in Belle. It pained Belle to return to Boston, but she knew that one day she would come back. As the song says, she left her heart in San Francisco.

Belle returned to Boston, hoping every day that Mr. Boalt Hall would make contact. About one year later, he did. Belle could not be contained! After several conversations, Belle began traveling to the Bay Area to see Mr. Boalt Hall. On her last trip, she found a little dog wandering the streets. She and Mr. Boalt Hall bonded with the dog and name him Kinshe, a mashup of both their names. Belle brought

Kinshe back to Boston, though he eventually ran away. Belle was very sad, but by 1975 she was ready to move to California.

Belle knew she needed her father's support if she was to move. She and her father went to the beach by the Oak Bluffs Vineyard Haven Bridge. They used to go there frequently to fish off the jetty or lie in the sand. There, she told her father of her decision to move to California and asked for his support. Papa Bear turned his body to face Belle and said, "I will just kill myself." He looked over at the bridge, low to the water, saying, "I will jump off that bridge." Belle looked up at the bridge and down toward the waterway, smiled at her father and said, "Oh, you'll be just fine, you're a good swimmer." They laughed, but a moment of seriousness followed. Papa Bear gazed at Belle through squinted eyes and asked if she is serious. She responded in the affirmative. Papa Bear began to cry, and so did Belle. They talked a while longer, and eventually (though with fear in his eyes), Papa Bear agreed.

Belle's father ruminated on all the times he had rescued Belle from her misadventures. Years before, he brought her and her then-husband, Richard, back to the island and then had to rescue her from Richard's abuse. Following her graduation from high school in 1970, he supported her financially until she found a job. In 1971, he helped her relocate away from Massachusetts when the death of her Grandmother Nina was too much to bear. Belle had wanted to move to New York near where she was born, but instead she ended up in New Jersey.

Her life in New Jersey in 1971 had been tumultuous. Belle received an offer to live with her ex-husband's family in the town of New Brunswick. She liked these people but did not know them well. After living with them for only a short time, Richard, her ex-husband, began coming around. He professed to have changed and wanted Belle back. Belle was vulnerable and took a chance with Richard. He bought her a little white dog, whom she named Cuddles, and moved Belle into a lovely apartment in Piscataway. They were together only a short while before Richard's violent ways returned. He locked Belle and Cuddles in the bedroom so she could not leave the house. Belle escaped through the window and ran away.

During this time, Belle worked at a bank. A certain customer was always asking to take her out. Belle called this customer after escaping through the window, and he rescued her from Richard. Now Belle was stuck with him. He was an older man and not Belle's type, but he did everything in his power to provide for her. Belle was very unhappy and knew she needed to get away. He was obsessed with Belle and wanted to marry her. Thankfully, Belle was still legally married to Richard. Belle contacted her father, who told her that she needed to leave New Jersey and return home. He promised to buy her a car and set her up again in Boston. He really wanted Belle to be close by and to consider going to college. Papa Bear was truly Belle's rescuer. He was everything to Belle and could not be replaced; he was a blessing from God, an earth-bound angel. Belle left New Jersey in 1972.

Belle returned to Boston to her own apartment with furnishings donated from various family members. Independent, she began to feel encouraged about her life. One weekend, she reunited with Paula and jokingly asked her move to Boston and share the apartment. To her surprise, Paula accepted. Belle did not really believe her, because they were never really close (Belle was closer to her older sister). About one month later however, during a horrific snow storm, Paula arrived in Boston in a U-Haul truck. Belle was in disbelief, but from that day forward she and Paula were inseparable, just as Belle had been previously with Reb. Paula and Belle lived life to the fullest together. It all began to slow down when Paula married and started a new life with her husband and sweet baby girl, Angela.

In 1975, Belle was twenty-six years old. She was young, adventurous, lively, and ready for change. She began the preparations to move to California. She completed her last semester at Northeastern University, then made arrangements to transfer to the University of San Francisco. She was ready to take the leap of faith and start a new life. What Belle would later realize was that this move would transform her life. The only internal conflict Belle still battled with was the fear of leaving her parents behind. Belle knew she needed this change and hungered for a life make-over. She wanted to be smart, educated, afford designer clothes, live comfortably, and most of all have her own financial security. Her driving force was to make her father proud, to be able to take care of both parents in their advanced years, become independent and stable, and prove Phyllis wrong.

In the spring of 1975, Belle was received in San Francisco by Mr. Boalt Hall. What a warm and wonderful reception he gave her! He drove her from the airport to a beautiful grouping of condominiums at the top of a big hill over a beautiful neighborhood. There Belle entered her first California apartment, which was totally amazing. The apartment had two bedrooms, was fully-furnished and colorful, had grass-like walls, and a large picture window overlooking the area of Diamond Heights. She thought to herself, *"What a gift, what a way to begin my life in California!"*

Belle was very thankful to Mr. Boalt Hall. Their relationship, though sometimes challenging, lasted for two years. In those two years, Belle reasserted herself in school, completed her Bachelor degree, was accepted into a Master's program, and worked as an accountant with the ILWU. She invested in her first car with the help of Papa Bear. Belle was proud of herself, and for the first time in her life Belle's father felt he can step back and just be a supporter rather than a rescuer. Belle jetted around in her little sports car with the drop top, dressed in her unique style that got her lots of attention. She finally felt good about herself. Belle realized that she was growing into herself; she was developing an inner understanding of self and a desire to be closer to God.

Early in 1977, Belle left Diamond Heights and moved to the Alameda Beach and Tennis Club in the East Bay over the Bay Bridge. This area was perfect, amazing. Belle had the beach across from her apartment and a lot of interesting black professionals as peers. It was the social ground for Belle's entertainment. There was always something going on. This was the first time Belle had lived alone and was able to provide for herself financially, though she still sent letters home asking Papa Bear for a little help. It was this move that initiated Belle's journey toward healing and forgiveness. She began to forgive herself for all the pain she suffered and for the challenging situations she endured. Though she led a fairly active social active life, Belle began to put God first. She worked diligently to improve her thoughts, decisions, and actions. California became her paradise for rebirth and emotional stabilization.

Although Belle was advancing and life was wonderful, her internal demons have not given up residence. Many of her most painful memories have never been directly revealed or discussed. In a way, Belle led a double life; she constructed a positive lifestyle and showed her academic brilliance, but she continued to feel insecure, especially in social situations.

Belle worked hard to further her learning, leaving limited time to catch up on social exposure. She found more security in small groups where she could shine with her beauty and grace but still hide behind her façade. Belle had great difficulty having conversations, but found that she was very versed in human behavior and could analyze situations and individuals. Belle's emotional imbalance and internal gaps showed through her lack of social exposure. We must remember that at twenty-eight, Belle was completing her BA; at thirty, she received her Master's in Psychology. Needless to say, this did not leave much time for social growth. Her ego further lost strength as the years passed, worsened by the fact that she had to play academic catch-up. Her past history only added to her lack of socialization and exacerbated her role as a victim. Although Belle was a noted academic scholar, she did not have the time to add social exactness to her repertoire of gifts. Belle saw herself through deceitful eyes, and she lived in two distinct worlds. She found more comfort in academics than in social settings. It was this security buffer that drove Belle to complete her Master's degree within one year and immediately apply for her doctorate program.

Belle's next stage of healing began when she achieved academic recognition. Being academically recognized bolstered her confidence and provided her with a sense of worldly accomplishment. Now a "valid" professional, she strove to be grammatically correct and articulate. However, she still did not feel confident in social conversations. Belle lacked the involvement and environment that those who attended college in their earlier years had been exposed to. What Belle did have, however, was an honest heart. People liked her. She was loyal, a great helper, a hard worker, engaging, funny, and a good dancer.

Doors opened. She found a great group of friends, received invitations to social gatherings, landed a great job, and then in 1977 met a great guy. This one was the man of her dreams, Mr. Sunshine. Belle fell immediately and deeply in love with him. She first saw him at a party she did not want to attend because she was too tired, but her friend convinced her to go. She didn't dress for the occasion and was not at her best. Not feeling confident in her appearance, she hung back in a dark corner of the party, observing others (something she always enjoyed doing). Suddenly the door opened and cast a bright light in from the hall. All Belle could see is the tall, exceedingly handsome guy with the brilliant smile coming through the doorway. He could not see her because she was in the dark; or so she thought.

Before she knew what is happening, he approached her and introduced himself. Belle almost melted. She was in total awe. They established a friendship, then a relationship that lasted six years. Belle lived the life she always envisioned, and she thanked him and his family for that chance. Belle so enjoyed him, his family, and all his friends. The relationship transformed Belle's life. She traveled, met amazing people with whom she would have lasting relationships, attended the best events, embraced her relationship with Mr. Sunshine's mother and father, and was exposed to incredible new experiences. For this period of time, Mr. Sunshine was Belle's knight in shining armor. What made him most amazing was that he *chose* Belle. The relationship did not last as long as Belle may have wanted, but it was this relationship that brought her out of the dark and into the light. She recognized that God brought Mr. Sunshine into her life to heal and transform her, and she thanked him for that every day.

In 1982, the relationship ended. Belle was heartbroken. She drank heavily for months and entered a deep depression. Life stopped and flat-lined again. Time passed, and Belle allowed her demons to return; everything she touched tarnished and broke. Though her life had taken a turn for the absolute worst, she maintained a sense of hope. She had yet to realize the gift of healing that she would soon receive. There are no mistakes when you walk with God. Belle's prayers for healing and forgiveness were in preparation for this moment. Although her days were spent in a depressed state, she spoke to God and began to read the Bible in a search for peace and healing. Belle knew that this was the end of her search for loving relationships; she now sought a relationship with God. Belle would never engage in a love relationship again.

Her next stage of healing came when Belle returned to church. This healing was so intense that Belle awakened on many nights to her bed shaking. She attributed this phenomenon to her recent prayers and active study of the Bible. Belle's next relationship was with God, and it was the best relationship of all. In him, Belle found spiritual guidance. She eventually realized that the breakup in 1982 was the fall she needed to begin her lifelong journey into self-sufficiency.

This was the fall that would cleanse and transform her. This was the true beginning of Belle.

Throughout this process, Belle's life continued to challenge her. She was unable to find work, her finances dwindled, and opportunities refused to present themselves. One night during prayer, Belle asked why things had become so difficult. She immediately realized that she might have to go home to her parents. This upset her, but she knew it was probably the truth.

Belle resisted God's push for her to return to Massachusetts. Belle went home for Christmas of 1985 and asked her parents what they wanted for Christmas. Separately, they both answered, "For you to come home." Belle knew this was what God wanted. She was despondent, but knew she had no option. Her time in California had come to an end. Belle conceded and let her father make the arrangements to move her furnishings, her dog (Rasta), and her car to Massachusetts. Belle knew this was God's plan because her life was falling apart. Within a month the movers arrived, and Belle and her dog left. After twelve years of joy, it was back to Massachusetts. However, Belle returned a different person: stable, educated, and employable.

Belle, now thirty-five years old, returned to her mother's until she could reestablish herself. She would not move back to Martha's Vineyard; Phyllis had made that very clear. After one year of struggling, Belle began work with a local college who allowed Belle to use their students for her dissertation study. Once settled at the college, Belle decided that she wanted a baby. She was getting older and was not married or in a relationship; in a word, she was stuck. She planned to go to a sperm bank, but she wanted her child to know her Cape Verdean culture.

One day, Belle talked to a very dear friend about going to the sperm bank. He was a special friend, a Cape Verdean born in Senegal, and a great person from a wonderful family. He offered to be the father of Belle's baby. Belle was excited and immediately proposed they try to get pregnant in January because her baby must be born in September, near Grandma Nina's birthday, or early October, which was Belle's birthday. So they did.

On October 13, 1987, the greatest healing of all took place. Belle gave birth to her beautiful daughter, Chantal. This changed Belle's world. Her life started to clear, all her demons were asked to come forward, and Belle began the process of ridding herself of the emotional toxins that had kept her trapped and disempowered for so many years. Belle found strength in the love from her parents, the birth of her beautiful daughter, and God. It was a process achieved.

While pregnant, Belle began her formal career as a therapist. One year after Chantal's birth, Belle bought her first house and a new Mercedes Benz. Amazingly, her father divorced Phyllis. He found out that she had stolen all his money and cleaned out all his bank accounts. Papa Bear moved out of the main house and into his cottage, ending the miserable chapter that was his life with Phyllis. He spent many nights with Belle, especially now that Chantal was there. In 1992, Belle built two houses on Martha's Vineyard; a main house and a cottage. This was where she would live out her life.

This was Belle's healing journey. However, let there be no mistake; her intruders would always try to reclaim their residence. Healing does not end with the 5-Key System. Rather, this system becomes a lifestyle. What is implanted through the 5-Key System is an internal alert mechanism that warns against a potential invasion; in effect, it is an installed heart light that guides you into clarity of thought and feeling, a heightened coping and protective system that provides immediate response and rescue. Belle called this her Papa Bear rescue system.

The lifelong aspect of the 5-Key System can be seen with Belle in February of 2016. At this time, Belle was vacationing in Cape Verde. Dogs ran freely and lived an independent existence free of the animal control regulations seen in the United States. The dogs ran in groups, sniffing and attempting to hump female dogs. One female dog fought them off and ran away, but the male dogs pursued her aggressively. Belle stopped on her walk to watch the dynamics. She got the feeling that she should protect the female dog. As she continued to watch, nausea washed over her and she realized the dogs were trying to rape the female dog. For an instant, Belle was transported back to the time of her own rape. Belle felt a sudden cringing in her body, and angry emotions began to surge. Immediately, Belle's internal alert and coping management systems engaged to protect her from these sensations and help her achieve clarity in her thoughts and feelings.

Thanks to her healing journey, Belle was eventually able to control these emotional intruders and prevent them from reestablishing residence in her now effectively managed cubicles. Through the healing process, she learned to recognize suppressed memories and took responsibility for the emotional intruders. She found forgiveness for all the negative occurrences in her life. More importantly, Belle forgave herself for what she once thought was her fault. She was able to ascertain and bring understanding to related feelings of blame, guilt, and shame. These four emotions—fault, blame, guilt, and shame—are what emotional intruders feast upon. It is easy to acknowledge uncomfortable events and the people involved in them, but if we do not identify the source of deeply embedded conflict, we will never release our emotional toxins. It is vitally important to identify these emotions within each area of discomfort.

Let's look at what happens when you believe an adverse event to be your fault. The definition of fault rings of failure, character weakness, something that impairs or is defective, and the deserving of blame and guilt. Fault indicates that there is an impairment in our character and in our judgment, thus impeding our cognitive abilities. Fault is the thought process that inhibits good decision making, thereby forming a layer of emotional density and confusion.

When Belle was raped, she could only think that she should not have been drinking. This laid heavily on her she blamed herself for the crime of another. She blamed herself too for leaving with a stranger who was years older simply because she did not want to go back to her mother's house drunk. Belle had met this man previously in the company of friends; he was very handsome and her friends seemed to like him. He was seven years older than she and her peers, and he supplied them alcohol. When he invited Belle to go to his apartment to sober up, she felt gratitude; she did not know that this would be the end of her innocence. Belle blacked out, only to awaken to the man raping her. She was devastated, and blamed herself for drinking and going with an older man to his apartment. She did not put his actions at fault, only her lack of good decision making. Strangely, he walked Belle home after the rape and treated her as if she was special. Belle, who had never even been kissed, immediately feel into his trap and shifted all blame away from him. She really believed that he wanted her, which was a new experience for her. For some time thereafter, every visit to her mother ended at his apartment.

This was Belle's first lesson in being sexually enslaved by a man. This was how she learned to have relationship with the opposite sex.

Let's examine Belle's course of blame. The definition of blame invokes taking responsibility for an affliction, deserving displeasure, or being the cause of a situation. Blame is similar to fault, except in that blame adds the component of accountability. Belle felt that she was the cause of the rape because she could not remember leaving the man's couch and going to his bed. She felt she must have gone along with him. Belle had never experienced "making out" before because boys were not attracted to her and she did not have access to her peers because of Phyllis' strict control. Without this frame of reference, she began to think that maybe she had made out with Benny—her rapist—and that it had led to her being raped. She blamed herself, thinking that she somehow must have asked for this to happen.

Guilt is a confusing meshwork of all colors. The definition of guilt reflects awareness of doing something wrong, unresolved regrets, and contribution to negative events. Guilt adds the component of willful wrongdoing, implying consciousness of an action or event. Belle's guilt was enhanced by her moral goal of wanting to save herself for her future husband, unlike her sexually active friends. Her guilt following her rape was exacerbated by the feeling that she had disappointed her father. Because Belle had never had a healthy relationship with a boy, nor did she have openly loving relationships with her family, she was an easy catch for a predator. Once she learned how to make men happy, she learned very quickly how to receive fleeting attentions.

Shame is a major contender. The definition of shame reflects painful feelings of disgust and disgrace, a sense of failure, condemnation, and a conscious sense of worthlessness and wrongdoing. Many valuable studies have examined the idea of shame. Shame is the internal indicator for feelings of worthlessness. Every time Belle had a sexual relationship, it confirmed her lack of worth. These exploitive behaviors brought Belle years of oppression. Being from Cape Verde, Belle grew up in a culture where one's shame could impact one's entire family. It was a firm rule to keep family matters in the family and not to bring *vergonha*, or shame, into the open. Doing so would cause a serious disconnect between the family and the person who defied the rule. With this in mind, how could Belle tell her parents that she had been drunk, had gone with an older man to his apartment alone, had had sex? She could tell no one. Her world was destroyed and she began to believe that Phyllis was right about her. Shame was the intravenous nourishment to her pain.

The ingredients of fault, blame, guilt, and shame create a recipe for internal vulnerability and a lifestyle of persistent internal turbulence. This turbulence consumes our moods, causes emotional imperfections, and takes proprietorship over our mere existence. This does not mean that you will not excel in your desires, nor does it mean that you will remain in a constant stop, block, or flat-line cycle. However, the emotional variables between stopping, blocking, and flat-lining with an influx of fault, blame, guilt, and shame cause internal congestion, which will always be working in the background and disturbing the healing process.

Belle received her restoration through self-discovery. Every positive experience (e.g., receiving her first "A," moving to California, building a relationship with God, excelling in academics, having her daughter) brought about a deeper understanding and self-confidence. Belle replaced her secrets with the telling of her story; she exchanged internal torment for forgiveness, her destructive behaviors for walking with God, her emotional inconsistencies with taking responsibility for her actions, and her lack of self-esteem with ability and experience with which she could help others navigate their own emotional turbulence.

The Key of Emotional Restoration

Remember the full instructions for Key 2 Restore, is in the corresponding workbook. Please read the entire workbook before proceeding with the emotional detox. The restorative and healing process consists of eight keys, outlined below:

I. Tell your story. Do not live with these radicals; let go of the pain. It is easier to experience pain in the short term than struggle with it for a lifetime.

II. Forgive yourself first. Finding forgiveness is the key that opens the door to the healing process.

III. Confront your internal turmoil. Break down the walls that are holding you captive.

IV. Recognize the truth of past events. Process these events until all truths have been uncovered, disclosed, and documented. Do not fear accessing pain; dig deep into your emotional banks and pull out all the emotional toxins.

V. Analyze and release the four emotional congestions: Fault, Blame, Guilt, and Shame. These have the capacity to block, stop, and flat-line. Reach complete understanding and acknowledgement of these congestions.

VI. Rewrite your story.

VII. Engage in self-discovery.

VIII. Rebuild your empowerment platform and position yourself anew.

The healing process involves eight keys to connect your feelings into a symphony in Oneness. Follow the steps below to begin this process.

I. In the workbook page provided, *8 Keys to Healing*, or in your private journal, outline the eight healing keys. Create your dialogue for each issue confronting these keys.

II. List the healing that occurred through the Cleansing process (e.g., relief of depression).

III. Write a letter to yourself about your healing process experience. Be sure to make note of any strong or meaningful emotions. If at a loss for how to begin, use the following template: *Dear Me, I now know that what happened (name the situation/people involved) was not my fault. I am not to blame for this (event); I will not carry guilt any longer, and I will not feel shame for (reason). However, I will take responsibility for (action). I have experienced a deep internal surge of relief, and am now ready to move forward from this (repeat situation/people involved) using my internal coping strategies of (list the coping strategies).* Include in the letter your feelings and reactions. This letter should be written after each event is addressed.

IV. Create a list of events you now understand and come to an awareness of the actions that occurred. This is a difficult task, so move slowly; reach out to your support system if need be. It is important to reveal your vulnerability and create your platform of strength and power. Create your evolution plan: "*The Me I Am Going To Be*."

V. Film a video of yourself describing your evolution out of emotional contamination. Write down your recipe for coping and reaching success. Remember that in order to heal, we must replace old images with new ones with purpose and value.

VI. Create an affirmation list, a poetic verse, dramatic rendition, or any form of positive expression to show how you have taken responsibility for the events in your life—not only the emotionally distressing events, but also daily ones (*e.g., with colleagues, work, family, friends, children*).

VII. Create a forgiveness list using the following script: "I forgive _____ (person[s]) for ______ (situation). Deep in my heart and through everything I believe in, I understand that _____, and I am ready to forgive and move forward." For every blocked or stopped memory, pen this notation of forgiveness. Remember to search deeply into the situation and be intent about forgiving even the smallest of emotional experiences. Do not pass over an experience that causes a little cringe of emotion; address it so it does not grow into a more pronounced emotional intruder. This is the process of cleaning out the emotional cubical that has stored so much negative emotional data.

VIII. Create your "Symphony in the Key of Oneness" story template:

Create the heading, "Healing." This is a skeletal key that will help you create your success plan. For each blocked and stopped emotion, fill in your template with your success recipe (e.g., Recipe for Social Adequacy: 10 lbs. of smiles, 3 tbsp. of conversation, a pinch of warmth). Conclude each recipe with directions for preparation (e.g.,

Mix all ingredients by stirring softly with loving hands. Pour out to the world). Once you have created your template, memorize each recipe. Visualize their existence in body, mind, and spirit, and reward yourself with a healing gift. This template creates an accessible system for installing emotional data, serving as a simple visual aid for coping and promoting ongoing healing.

This system was created to allow for healing and restoration. It will become your template for keeping harmful events from reattaching themselves to your life. It is important to allow the purity of your birth to not be diminished and to recognize the blessing you hold within. Your greatness is to be realized and not compromised. As for Belle, her faith in God permeates all that she does; this is the glue that now holds her together. It is imperative that you find your own spiritual belief system and incorporate it into your healing process.

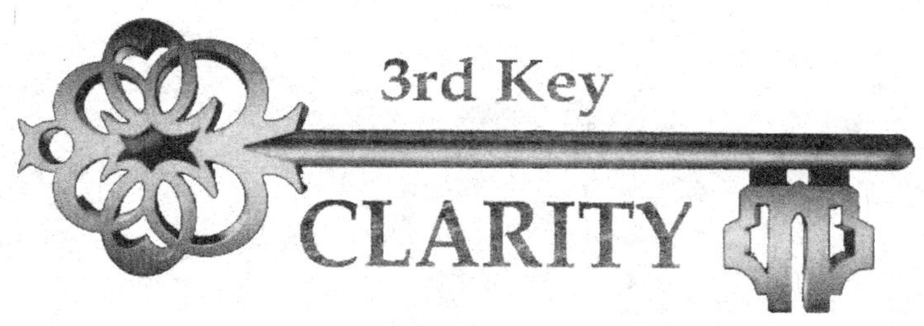
3rd Key
CLARITY

Chapter 4

KEY# 3
CLARITY AND WISDOM KEY

To find emotional clarity, we must create an uncluttered and vibrant channel that allows input and output to stream through our conscious and unconscious mind with emotional balance. To find clarity, we must seek wisdom. Clarity is the "aha" moment of our 5-Key System. It is the filter through which any lingering toxins will pass during excavation. Keys 1 and 2 in our emotional detox system cleansed and healed most of our emotional baggage; now it is time to fine tune and begin the rehabilitation process toward emotional wisdom.

Belle's Journey through Clarity

Belle found clarity in the birth of her daughter, Chantal. Belle had carried a hidden fear that she was cursed and would never have children. At thirty-six years of age, she took control of this fear and began her own journey toward conception. After a few attempts without positive results, however, she felt her fears had been confirmed. This made her decide to consult a reproductive endocrinologist, or an infertility specialist. At her first appointment, however, she tested positive for pregnancy. When she received the results, Belle felt a sense of total digestion and assurance. It was like the toxins had begun to evacuate her body.

However, Belle did retain some fears regarding her past "worldly" lifestyle. She feared that some type of punishment for her past would come to curse her unborn child. Flashbacks danced through her mind and filled her every thought. However, rather than succumbing to emotional recontamination as she would have in the past, becoming distracted and overwhelmed, Belle instead felt a lightness in her body. At this moment, Belle experienced a moment of forgiveness and felt ownership over her experiences; these memories would no cause pain, but rather give her a promise of eternal healing. This marked Belle's self-forgiveness and newness of mind and thought. In this moment, Belle finally reached internal understanding. She was at last able to bridge her past pain with her newly derived passions to channel a deeper emotional understanding of herself. This sparked her journey into achieving emotional wisdom. She found meaning and purpose in her life. Her pregnancy went extraordinarily well, and her baby girl was born healthy and beautiful. For Belle, this was her epiphany to Oneness; her life had been given a significant purpose and vision. Belle pregnancy gave her clarity, which allowed her to live in the sanctity of emotional wisdom.

Let's examine clarity as a way to achieve emotional wisdom. Clarity and wisdom work together to give us a clear and concise understanding of all things possible; they become tools that lend the bearer an instinctive grasp of any challenge or situation. This complete evolutionary integration of body, mind, and spirit create the symphonic key of Oneness. It is an organic measurement for life and living that gives us the ability to trust and rely on our intuitive powers. Imagine retaining your sense of innocence while enjoying a self-sufficient, autonomous manifestation of self.

When we are cluttered with unresolved memories—especially those that stop, block, and flat line—we tend to be less able to actualize emotional clarity. This means that clarity is difficult to access if the first two steps of the 5-Key System have not been followed. If this system does not fit you, you should access another process or system that will allow you to disable your emotional toxins. Such a system should allow you to create a cognitive and emotionally protective mechanism that includes coping strategies, emotional intruder alerts, and a planned means of discharging any new emotional toxins.

When we achieve emotional clarity, we gain the ability to filter out negative emotions and rebound more effectively from negative input. Without clarity, we allow ourselves to encounter turbulence related to procrastination, ambivalence, and changes in mood, which affect and allow for intrusions that can harm our mental and physical health.

We are bombarded with various forms of input, output, and data on a daily basis. These challenges, some good and some not so good, elicit varying emotional responses. We live in a culture that requires us to attend, produce, create, follow societal norms, and meet societal obligations. We are amazing individuals, yet we do not allow ourselves to function at our full potential. We over or under eat, overuse substances in the name of social interaction, place ourselves in unimportant competitions (and often wonder why we make them so important), and become overly critical, overwhelmed, and analytical. We immerse ourselves in unimportant matters for unimportant reasons and achieve no gain. We wind ourselves up and propel ourselves forward and call this productivity, which we associate with balanced living. Ask yourself the question: who is really balanced? Those who have or those who have not? Let's not judge others, but instead look into ourselves.

An important motto to remember is "growth through inner experiences." If we are looking for balance, we need to look inside ourselves for the map. If we continue to live from the outside, we create habitats for emotional contaminants. To live knowing that these contaminants are present and planning their attack is to live feeling emotionally smothered. How much better it is to live life knowing that you have the power to intuitively and cognitively understand, envision, empathize, and resolve these issues! For this is living life in balanced harmony. Such harmony frees us from the physical, mental, and medical stresses that arise from emotional complications.

So how do we reach emotional wisdom? Proverbs 9:10 tells us that "The fear of the Lord is the beginning of wisdom, and the knowledge of the Holy One is insight." This is the purest form of wisdom. Emotional wisdom is the internal consciousness that evolves from embedded, unconscious, crippling emotions to a state of acceptance, understanding, and the filtration of negative emotional content. It is this deep, imprinted understanding of life's challenges that guides our interactions and responses. This is where integrity, purposeful living, and integrative relationships reside. When we are emotionally wise, we search deep within ourselves for our personal truth and seek out the innate gifts that were given to us at birth. With this newly reconditioned emotionality, we begin to approach our world differently, associate with others in deeper understanding, create integrative thoughts and responses, build effective relationships with intent and meaning, and live a life of purpose. Imagine being able to see with clear vision and think from a place of wisdom!

We have discussed traumatic events that leave a wake of turbulence and torment. We must now add to our emotional web the soft, dormant moments related to our parents and their parenting, any bonding issues, sibling relationships, and loss of loved ones. It can be easy to normalize these memories as typical "family issues," but we must not underestimate how they can cause intense pain, binding us and holding hostage. As children, we idealize our parents and place all our emotional vitality and trust into these relationships. We learn from these relationships, and they become a serious part of our characters and development. For some, these relationships have limited complications; for others, the complications are intense.

Let's return to Belle's example. Belle idealized her father. He was her hero, and while she loved her mother, they never formed an internal bond—rather, their relationship was one of functional caregiving. Because of this, Belle constantly sought out mother figures throughout her life—figures who would cook and do her hair and help her with her homework. Belle's mother was too sick to do these things. As Belle developed, she feared that she might become like her mother and never achieve her desires or passions. Belle felt that her mother had much unexplored potential, such as becoming an English teacher (shown by how she always corrected Belle's terrible grammar). Belle most appreciated her mother's incredible beauty and her love for music. The two used to travel by bus from state to state to buy music albums; her mother loved big band, jazz, and Cape Verdean *morna* (slow) music. Belle preserved her mother's record collection, including one of her mother singing a Cape Verdean song. Belle always felt that if her mother and father had stayed together, her mother's life would have been very different.

Belle idealized her father until she was old enough to realize that he had cheated on her mother with Phyllis. Belle's mother later told Belle that it was not her father's fault. She told Belle that she was extremely fearful of getting pregnant again so she stopped having sex with Belle's father. However, years after her father's death in 1997, Belle found an assortment of letters written by her mother that her father kept. These letters were apparently written when Belle was very young. The letters were so heart-wrenching that Belle could only get through two. She read of her mother's desperation in asking for financial help, signs that she must have gone through terribly difficult times because Belle always knew her mother to resist asking anyone for help, especially Belle's father. Belle's heart broke for her mother, but she did not want to be mad at her father. The letters distorted her view of him, but could not alter the love she felt.

Until her mother's death in 2015, Belle grew closer to her and began to see her through different eyes. A few years before her death, Belle's mother told her, "Belle, I love you so much that it hurts." Belle had waited more than 50 years to hear this. In a full circle, Belle returned to her role as her mother's caretaker until the woman's passing at age ninety. For years prior to her mother's passing, Belle coordinated and supervised her mother's caregivers and spent every day with or in contact with her mother. She grew fond of her mother and began to understand her journey and the cause for her withdrawals from life. Caring for her mother during her times of vulnerability gave Belle intense healing, forgiveness, and understanding. The letters came at a time that helped Belle find empathy for her mother's emotional journey; she came to realize that her mother had suffered from blocked, stopped, and flat-lined emotions all her life without interruption. Belle thanked God for the gift of her mother's love. She knew with certainty that her mother always loved her. Receiving her mother's words of love during her last years helped Belle to heal; from this, she could enjoy a sense of freedom and greater familial attachment.

We receive the familial gifts of DNA and the emotional wisdom from past generations. Of course, we are also individuals endowed with our own characteristics that have been shaped by our external and internal influences. Finding our uniqueness and individuality is a challenge because we are not always (and in the case of some, never) aware of these influences and how they condition our thoughts, feelings, and reactions. In order to begin to understand our complex characteristic compositions, we need to examine the innate gifts given to us at birth, generational and cultural dispositions, predisposed genetics from our family trees, environments in which we have been immersed, and learned behaviors from outside sources. What is of upmost importance the understanding of our innate gifts. These gifts are our purest foundations, our internal truths, yet we do not always know how to access them. How many times have we been asked about our passions only to be unable to answer?

Going back to the example of Belle, she observed others' behaviors throughout her childhood to the point of obsession. Her staring could be so intense that people would threaten her, yell at her for looking at them, and want to physically confront her. Richard at times became irate at her staring and accused her of flirting, then would beat her and call her names as punishment. These threats and abuses did not stop her habit, however. From childhood to adulthood, she continued to learn about others by observing their behaviors. Later in life, her daughter, a twenty-nine-year-old medical student, told Belle that one day her staring would end in an unpleasant confrontation. Her daughter described these states of observation as trances.

Belle remained unaware of this behavior because it was a natural part of who she was. Eventually, these "obsessions" that others would have her suppress opened up a whole new world for Belle. Belle was now a highly recognized and sought after clinician, an expert in traumatic abuse and owner of a practice for more than twenty-six years. Her years of obsessive observation and study of psychology made her an amazing diagnostician. Belle connected her passions of behavioral observations, the innate gifts given to her at birth, with her mishaps and life lessons to eventually evolve and be able to heal others. Belle realized that her purpose was to experience the pains of life's lessons and apply them to her passion for observing behaviors, creating a vehicle for elevating wisdom and emotional healing.

We have to remember that we are born with the purity of wisdom. It lives within us, but over time it becomes woven into the fabric of life, absorbed, and replaced. Wisdom is an anthology of knowledge, understanding, experience, insight, and virtue. Achieving this depth of thought and expression can only occur once we have fallen and experienced the effects of block, stop, and flat-line. Hopefully, we can then begin to rise, face the truth of our life's challenges, and take control of our purpose.

It is important that we reveal to ourselves, from the purity of our hearts, our innate uniqueness, value, purpose, and creativity. It is our individual responsibilities to discover the truth in our pain, heal our wounds, and find the true meaning of our existence while weaving the fabric of emotional wisdom. We need to embrace the many hues of our colorful tapestry—even those that are not so beautiful—with a deep understanding of the tactile sensations interwoven into our life's pattern.

In summary, to achieve clarity and harvest the anthology of wisdom, we must first seek truth, allow for purity of heart, and intertwine our life's mishaps with our innate passions. This blending will create a bond between our past emotional challenges and our personal gifts. In Belle's case, her traumatic experience with rape allowed her to become an expert in child sexual abuse and use that position to help others. Who could do this better than Belle?

The Journey to Emotional Clarity

Remember the full instructions for Key 3 Clarity is in the corresponding workbook. Please read the entire workbook before proceeding with the emotional detox. Seek clarity and begin your journey toward wisdom using the following keys:

I. Create an "I believe" list, either in the workbook provided or your own. These beliefs should come from an insightful and true understanding of your past emotional challenges. Explore every belief related to each event to achieve complete clarity of each one.

II. Write a daily belief affirmation (*or repeat the same*) on a sticky note and place it on a surface that you visit often (*e.g., bedroom mirror, front door*). Read this affirmation aloud to instill it into your consciousness. Change these affirmations as new and deeper belief content emerges.

III. Create a Success Recipe Template (*an example is found in your workbook*). This template will help you redefine your purpose and internal data. For each "Blocker and Stopper" that you identified in the Cleansing chapter, you will fill in your template using each identified emotional challenge and create a success recipe. List the ingredients for success (*e.g., 10 lbs. of comfort, 15 lbs. of confidence*). Conclude with directions for preparation (*e.g., mix all ingredients, stir softly with loving hands, and pour out to the world*). Once you have created your template, memorize the recipe and visualize its existence in body, mind, and spirit. Reward yourself with a gift of deep understanding. The purpose of this template is to create an accessible system for inputting emotional data, visualizing coping mechanisms, and establishing ongoing clarity on your life's challenges.

Use the workbook provided to seek emotional wisdom through the following steps:

I. Create a video or an auditory presentation on self-trust. What do you trust about yourself? What do you still fear is deceiving about you? Record these thoughts and feelings. Remember this is just to assist in nurturing a deeper sense of self. Do not fear being honest, for honesty and truth are important keys for reaching purity of heart.

II. At the end of this recording, create a clarity of thought collage (*e.g., in words, pictures, poetry*). This collage should reflect your truths and deceptions. Then comment on your commitment to your deeper understanding of these truths and deceptions. For example, *I am committed to transitioning my way of____ to _____.*

III. Create your wisdom directory *(e.g., I lie to get my way but now I will divulge the truth to open my emotional awareness*).

IV. Remove the mask by creating a transparency script. This will require you to write your story and will allow you to see through indiscriminating eyes.

V. Evolve by creating a declaration of emotional evolution, like the following:

I, _______, do hereby acknowledge and declare that _________. I hereby irrevocably undertake the oath to ______________. I further undertake not to continue to allow __________. I hereby declare that I _________will continue to _________________in order to achieve total internal peace, harmony, and emotional wisdom and clarity. (Sign and date.)

VI. See through a new set of eyes by telling your new story through the eyes of wisdom.

VII. Compose your symphony in the key of Oneness by creating a musical verse that you can hum or sing easily. Use this to elicit an emotionally calming place of peace.

The deeper we seek admission into our toxic and cluttered holding tanks—the very same that were once blocked, stopped, and flat-lined—we evolve into a deeper sense of clarity and emotional wisdom. Our goal is to find clarity of mind, change our emotional input and output, and gain the ability to create new emotional destinations. This system will help you unmask your identifiable truths, nurture a passion for living to your highest potential, diminish any fear of looking inside and accessing your innate gifts, gain a full understanding of your emotional capacity, and grow into an emotional strength that is permanent.

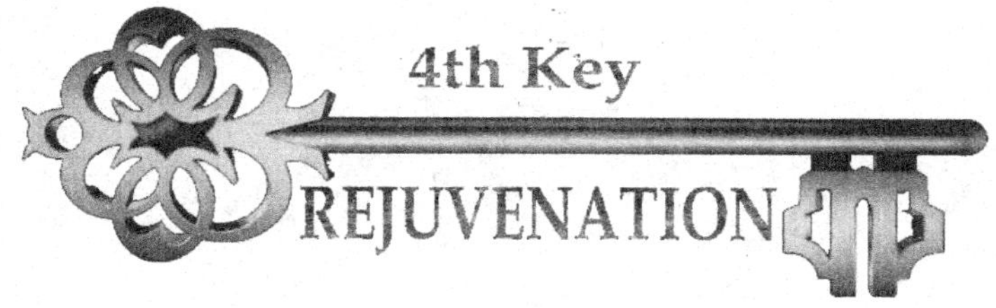
4th Key
REJUVENATION

Chapter 5

KEY# 4
REJUVENATION AND EMOTIONAL REBIRTH

Rejuvenation is the process that renews joy and lifts the spirit. The core of rejuvenation is a profound feeling of emotional freedom. It is from this core that we find appreciation for embracing and energizing moments. When we rejuvenate, we experience a sense of rebirth and revitalization. As part of our emotional detox journey, we will use this key to develop emotional cohesiveness by bridging our passions with our mishaps and enjoy a rebirth of emotional freedom.

Many years ago, I wrote a curriculum, *Bridging Passions with Mishaps*, for young adults exploring this process of emotional cohesion. It consisted of conversations created to impact young women facing life's daily challenges and desiring to create and sustain lifelong decisions. These decisions could refer to educational endeavors, career paths, building sustaining personal and professional relationships, mastering physical and financial wellness, and building a positive and powerful platform.

When journeying through life, we convene upon and prevail over many challenges. During our travels, we can be unaware of the inner gifts that have been born out of our passions and our mishaps. We have a propensity to overlook our passions and become wedged and misguided by our mishaps. Our passions relate to those sometimes small behaviors—minor idiosyncrasies and passing moments—from which we want more or find ourselves trapped in density. When we experience these moments fully, we evolve into a state of gratification, feel accomplishment, and hunger for further exploration. Mishaps can be momentous, and are often laden with mistakes, inadequacies, ego interruptions, anxieties, depressions, anger, grieving, and other such painful occurrences. The goal in this process is to bridge the innate—our inborn passions—to the inevitable—our unexpected mishaps.

By assessing, embracing, and bridging the known with the unexpected, we strengthen our power over life's decisions and convictions. Our personal evolution is not in error; we are predisposed to our destiny. Therefore, all that has passed, is in progress, and will come to pass is the inevitable. We need to formulate, pacify, nurture, and bridge this destiny. By linking our passions to our mishaps; our positives to our negatives; our strengths to our weaknesses; our gifts and talents to our hindrances and victimizations; we construct an individualized portfolio to help us experience emotional freedom. In the provided workbook, you will find the blueprint for *Bridging Passions with Mishaps.*

Belle's Journey through Rejuvenation

Belle's gifts intensified when she learned how to merge her passions with her mishaps. After she gave birth to Chantal, Belle began developing her clinical career, providing services for a fee at a mental health clinic. She had limited experience, but grew in the field quickly. After a short period of training and skills development, she was asked to join a select team being trained for child sexual abuse-related forensic evaluations. Belle was trained and supervised by the very best in the field. Within a short time, she gained recognition in the mental health arena, the court system, and the community. Her work to provide clinical treatment to those suffering from post-traumatic stress disorder extended long into the future, and she built a long history of working with sexual abuse survivors.

Belle found it interesting that she was desensitized to the disclosures and visualizations of sexually traumatic events, but had difficulty whenever the case involved a step-parent, especially a step-mother or an alleged pedophile. She began to screen her cases very carefully, and would not accept referrals for alleged pedophiles. Through her emotional detoxing journey and in learning to bridge her emotional blockage, stoppage, and flat-lining effects with her passions, Belle was able to establish a balanced system of emotional freedom.

After suffering three years with diabetes and renal failure, Belle's father died in 1997. This was traumatic for Belle, who loved her father more than life itself; she had lost her best friend, rescuer, and hero. Before falling ill, Papa Bear had helped Belle build her new home on Martha's Vineyard. He did all the brick work and built her a beautiful fireplace in her family room. During this time, a brick fell on his foot and the affected toe never healed. Life for Papa Bear began to decline quickly. In a very short period of time, he lost a toe, a leg, and a finger. Soon after, he required dialysis. This was a time of deep sorrow for Belle's family. Even with all this going on, Papa Bear's spirit remained hopeful.

Papa Bear began to use a prosthetic leg with the hope that he would regain some semblance of independence. He made many attempts to drive his newly bought Tolfeo automobile—a fully loaded limited edition of which he was very proud. On one occasion, he excitedly took Chappy, his trusted dog of fourteen years, Chantal, and Belle for a ride. Belle was also excited to see her father so happy. Everything was going well until he miscalculated a sharp turn. Belle feared the worst, but fortunately no cars approached from the opposite direction. Belle grabbed the wheel and Papa Bear adjusted his footing and put on the brake. After a deep breath, Belle asked her father if she should take the wheel, but his pride did not allow her to. Belle consented but suggested they take less driven roads. Papa Bear agreed and they arrived home safely.

Papa Bear's drive to find freedom from his debilitating illnesses was incredible. Every day, he created a new project. He was used to having workers and supervising a crew of men, so it was easy for him to transition into "boss" mode. The only problem was, Belle and Chantal were now his employees. Papa Bear loved his garden, but Belle had no patience for the delicate and concise manner with which he planted and maintained it (though she tried). Chantal loved doing everything with Papa Bear, so she became his main employee. Belle loved looking out the window and watching them interact; Papa Bear on his red rolling wagon that he pushed with one leg, Chantal holding her garden basket in hand.

One summer, I visited from California. Papa Bear was intent on building a grape trellis, insistent that Belle and Chantal should have one. David and I followed Papa Bear's comprehensive instructions while he sat in his wheelchair reviewing his plan. His mind was amazing; he loved the world of geometry and was a perfectionist. Even after his death, he left Belle with many memories. Every late summer following his death, when the grapes would begin to show growth, Belle would remember the day he built the trellis and embrace the memories of her father. The grapevine also memorialized Grandma Nina, who had always grown the same juicy concord grapes. It would later become clear to Belle that Papa Bear had been focused on completing everything he had planned for Belle and Chantal's home before his health declined. He had concentrated on all that needed to be done so that Belle and Chantal would be comfortable. In this way, Papa Bear had continued his role of rescuer even in his most despairing times.

Eventually, Papa Bear became weak and lost his mobility. Belle took on the role of his caretaker, and was very protective of her father. She endured every aspect of his suffering and used every resource available to create a comfortable and dignified environment for him. Papa Bear, who loved traveling, dressing up, cooking, playing his guitar and piano, golfing, and fishing, could no longer enjoy these pastimes. He became quiet, sometimes angry, and very frustrated with how life had changed course. His hope of independence dwindled and he began to settle into despair and hopelessness. This was not the man Belle knew; she deeply felt his sense of despair and realized that she had to stop working to take better care of him. She did not want to be away from him, but her work took her off the island all day every day.

In 1993, four years into building her home on Martha's Vineyard, Belle resigned from her job off the island with hopes of creating a lucrative income on Martha's Vineyard. She had her car payments, a mortgage for a house she owned off the island, and the two homes she had built on Martha's Vineyard. Despite these daunting facts, she had faith that God would help her find her way. For a short while, things were challenging. She sold the house off the island in order to maintain everything else. Gifted with tenacity and endurance, Belle eventually became the clinician in two schools on the island, opened her private practice, and formed a contract with a mental health agency off the island to open and manage a clinic for them on Martha's Vineyard. Belle continued in this capacity until her father passed.

In 1997 when her father died, Belle's grief was intense. Her saving grace was Chantal, without whom Belle might have gone along with her father. She experienced fear and anxiety as she had never navigated life without him. All her decisions had been made with her father's advice and acceptance. She wondered who would rescue her, who would love her unconditionally, and who would protect her. She began to question her abilities and feared taking on life's responsibilities without her father's help. He had been her coach, mentor, best friend, and loving parent. Still, she knew he had suffered enough, what with his health issues and with the pain caused by Phyllis leaving him to die a poor man. Belle's anger escalated as she thought of how her father had done so much for so many, especially Phyllis, but was forced to leave the earth in pain.

Once Belle had buried her father, she entered survival mode swiftly. Although competent in business matters, she felt lost without her father. Her emotional freedom was challenged; losing her father was the most painful event she had ever experienced. The image her father, helpless in a casket, traumatized her. Fortunately, Chantal, then ten years old, helped Belle through her healing process. Belle realized the impact her time spent caring for her father had had, though she would do it again, and how it had interrupted her parenting of Chantal. Neither she nor Chantal had realized how much time his care had taken from their relationship. Belle had always tried to balance her time with Chantal and Papa Bear, but it was different after his passing. In missing him, they grew even closer. In a way, Belle took on the role with Chantal that she had once enjoyed with her father. This gave her a strong sense of emotional freedom through her loss.

Papa Bear's passing brought Belle and Chantal ever closer. Chantal possessed the innate gift of wisdom. She understood emotions and attachments well, but was not overly emotionally expressive herself. Though Belle and Chantal shared moments of grief together, Belle harbored an internal discomfort that pushed her toward her old, unhealthy habits for coping with pain. Belle knew that if she allowed these toxic intruders to re-enter and take hold, it would destroy her and change Chantal's life. So, Belle dealt with her pain, found strength though meeting her daily obligations and responsibilities, and embraced the gift that God had given her—Chantal. Her life, the two major emotional events within her life, the birth of her daughter, and the death of her father had built in Belle a strong relationship with God and a rebirth of her innate passions.

Emotional freedom requires a detox process that lends the ability to confront, challenge truths, and find forgiveness. There are many techniques that assist in finding emotional freedom. The EFT tapping technique is a powerful modality similar to acupuncture but without the use of needles. This process is used to help with achieving emotional freedom. Hypnosis is another technique used to assist this process Many trained practitioners offer these treatments. There are also spiritual processes, such as meditation and yoga. These are all recognized emotional freedom techniques. When choosing a technique, it is important to remove unnecessary emotional burdens from your internal drive and cultivate a positive processing approach to access positive realities. This will enhance your ability to maintain a state of emotional freedom.

Let's visit the idea of emotional rebirth. In this process, we release all emotional toxins and establish stability. Once these negative emotions have been evacuated, confronted, realized, and forgiven, we enter the rebirthing process. This process simulates the gift of life; we release the weight of our toxic emotions and work from a place of strength to establish base transparency. This removes destructive emotions, leaving only those emotions that complement your passions, desires, and strengths. Through the rebirthing process, a part of the 5-Key System, we begin to experience a surge of internal energy that seeks newness, creativity, and spiritual fluidity.

Belle's rebirth began in 1999 when she found God. She began to understand her clients and their journeys very deeply. During her clinical sessions, Belle often felt her client's pain so acutely that they asked if she was clairvoyant. Belle was intuitive, but it was her life experiences that had shaped her clinical ability. Her relationship with God also provided her with the words, feelings, and visions that helped her perform clinical healing.

In 2003, Chantal and Belle temporarily moved off the island so that Chantal could attend a private high school. They would return to the island on weekends and for the summers. Since they were going to do this for the four years of high school, Belle decided to open her private practice in the city where she once lived. Her first office was directly across the street from her mother's old house. She created a nonprofit organization, which she named after Grandma Nina, in the community she wanted to help. Her certification as a minority- and woman-owned business allowed her to acquire difficult contracts and grants. She also became a participant on many insurance panels for third-party insurance billing. She opened her clinic doors to her community, and would continue to provide therapeutic services long into the future.

In 2006, Chantal graduated from high school at the top of her class. She chose George Washington University for a pre-med major. Belle was alone now, but not lonely. She worked diligently to build her business. She felt the strength of her father and grandmother inside her, driving her. She lived according to the image that she had visualized many years prior. She was content, powerful, and impressed by her endeavors and abilities. She experienced emotional rebirth and felt the power of accepting, appreciating, and enjoying her Oneness.

During the rejuvenation process, we should be mindful of how our emotions and health relate. It is important to restructure our emotional input and release all negative toxins before they find a gathering place and begin to affect our health. We have to remember: when we are emotionally charged, we inflict biological tension on our bodies. When we find peace with our emotions, we enhance our ability to revive and improve our health.

Also important in this revival is learning to love and embrace ourselves. This natural state of loving oneself is not the same as accepting the emotionally toxicity embedded in one's identity. We have to find the divide between what is real and what has simply taken up residency. Sometimes this is difficult, and it requires clarity of thought, word, and action. To reclaim self-love, we must become our positive characteristics. We must expose our inner strengths and our ability to balance our emotions and tendencies.

When identifying your virtues, become cognitively aware of your characteristics. For instance, Belle identifies her virtues as caring, simplistic, flexible, intuitive, understanding, and respectful to others. This shows us that Belle feels strongly when these virtues are under attack, which can change her characteristic reactions. When you think of your virtues, you will begin to understand how others can trigger negative responses from you. For instance, Belle's strongest virtue is respect; she requires that others respect her as she respects them. When there is an occasion of disrespect, Belle becomes agitated and feels an immediate need to confront the issue and find a solution.

Belle knows that if she contains the response, she will become anxious, angry, and consumed. Her confrontation reduces her discomfort and immediately quells the conflict. You will find that your habitual, ingrained personality traits, those that are a part of growth and development, are the authors of your covert and overt presentations. Through the detoxing system, you have learned how to reconstruct, negotiate, visualize, and feel your emotions. You have groomed these traits and revitalized their performance. Even when groomed and manicured, however, these traits can suffer change when presented negatively by others. When Belle observes or experiences a situation disrespectful to herself or others, for example, she is trigged to take action and can become incensed. The path to loving yourself, finding your balance, and appreciating internal peace changes how you react to these situations.

The Journey to Emotional Rejuvenation

Remember the full instructions for Key 4 Rejuvenation, is in the corresponding workbook. Please read the entire workbook before proceeding with the emotional detox. The keys to rejuvenation, rebirth, and emotional freedom are as follows:

I. Finding Emotion Freedom

- Confront emotional intrusions
- Challenge truths
- Allow for forgiveness

II. Emotional Rebirth and Revitalization

- Begin to create a transformation
- Experience of a spiritual flow
- Experience a newness of thought and feeling

III. Bridge Passions with Mishaps

- Achieve emotional cohesiveness

IV. Loving Yourself

- Evolution of personality traits
- Finding balance
- Identifying triggers

Emotional freedom is a major key to rejuvenation. Imagine having the freedom to feel, express, and understand your emotions without constraint. In this process, we must allow for and accept change. There has to be a conscious, thought out action and execution for change to occur. We must find clarity in this process, acknowledge and accept our previous emotional inputs and responses, and develop a sense of harmony, loyalty, and honesty towards ourselves. Throughout this process, be mindful of your natural reactions; know how to separate what you want from what you need, examine the *whole* you, practice moderation and set clear boundaries, and embrace yourself through healthy interactions.

5th Key
TRANSFORMATION

Chapter 6

KEY# 5
TRANSFORMATION THROUGH EMOTIONAL JUBILATION

"I was 4 years old when Dr. Celina came into my life. I am now 19. As a young boy, my three siblings and I were removed from our mother's care because of her drug use and my father wanted nothing to do with me. My pain turned into anger and my life became very complex. Dr. Celina never gave up on me. When I was a walking pharmacy, she stood by me and helped the doctor's remove unneeded medications. When I was involved in the court system because of acting out behaviors, she helped the court system understand my pain. When I cried out for my parents, she communicated with my family members to help them understand my cry. Today, I am finishing my second year of college and looking forward to a career as an engineer.

Dr. Celina you do not know how much I appreciate you. You are always there for me. Without you, I would not be who I am today. I thank you for your consistency. I thank you for you believing in me. I thank you for changing my life. I now have the tools to move forward and believe in myself."

Emotional transformation like the one above is a series of mindful steps toward emotional stability. The key to transformation is mindfulness, through which we create an insightful and reflective channel for awareness and understanding. We cannot forget that it is the bad times, the intensely negative experiences, that create in us a disposition for change. No matter the cause of our pain, we all seek remedies. However, many of these remedies are not effective because we do not know how to create emotional balance.

Belle's Journey to Transformation

In 2009, Belle realized she had transformed. She had embraced her life experiences and believed that her past sufferings had a divine purpose. She grew into self-appreciation and realized that without all she had endured, she would not be the caring, confident, and talented person that she was. For Belle, her tranquility came once her daughter was well settled on her academic journey and Belle's clinical expertise was recognized and accepted. Most important for Belle was her achievement of total independence. Belle depended upon Belle alone, and she did so with a confidence, clarity, and wisdom that she had never before experienced.

For eighteen years, Belle had exceeded her own expectations. She never could have imagined the gifts awaiting her. Once she internalized her gifts, she opened doors that she never expected she could open. Belle's greatest gifts were her instinctive appreciation for her clinical journey and her ability to deeply understand the pain of others.

To achieve transformation, we must travel beyond our conscious awareness and seek true wisdom. Arrival at this transitional abode requires a process of forgiveness, healing, and rebirth. Then, through this process, we achieve transformation. It is also important to remember that to unburden our emotional content, we must have instilled in ourselves the coping and managing tools for balancing new emotional imbalances. Imagine experiencing a daytime walk in a spirit of lightness, seeing though clear eyes and mind, receiving clarity rather than distraction, and rerouting internal diversions to their proper direction. What a relieving, revitalizing, and transforming way to live!

Remember the full instructions for Key 5 Transformation, is in the corresponding workbook. Please read the entire workbook before proceeding with the emotional detox. Your arrival at this key in the 5-Key System indicates that you have reached an understanding of your emotional subconscious, internal functioning, and external purpose. Transformation is a magical key whereby you learn how and when to extract a positive emotion from a negative one. For example, the positive reversal of anger is passion. Understanding this kind of emotional energy enhances our ability to reverse negative emotions. Just as energy attracts like energy, focusing on emotional lightness will bring it out of the depths of emotional heaviness. If you believe this, you can manifest and transition emotional energy to control many aspects of your responses to life challenges. Throughout this 5-Key System and journal, you have been prompted to embody emotional Oneness by creating and strengthening your emotional balance. The visualization process in this system was the key to creating new energy. The greater key to transformational success is within you; you are the author, editor, and publisher of your life story.

When we achieve transformational success, we realize the ability to cope with and manage our emotions. We learn how to visualize and energize our dreams and find ourselves inspired and motivated toward higher achievements. When seeking success, we often lack understanding and purity of thought, feeling, and action; we focus on what is readily available and easily attainable rather than what is in our larger realm of achievement. I am always amazed by the effort we put into achieving a lesser reward for instant gain rather than building upon our already innate gifts and passions. We lose so much from depending upon the tangible. We raise thoughts, emotions, visions, and beliefs that are disempowering. To achieve total transformation into emotional Oneness, you must change your negative thoughts, perceptions, and practices. You are your author, editor, and publisher, so write yourself a bestseller!

Positive thoughts and perceptions bring about positive practices and executions. Do not head for easy street; embrace a challenge and divorce your fear of failure or of being exposed. Expose yourself and experience the empowerment of you. Remember that your gifts have been cultivated through your life experiences and the pain associated with them.

Belle's lifelong vision was to independently create a successful path and career where she would thrive and be her own boss. After years of pain, she began working toward success and living out her vision. When in graduate school at the University of San Francisco, she lived in a beautiful area of Berkeley Hills. Prior to this, she had always lived in luxury apartments in San Francisco and Alameda. In the Berkeley Hills, she embraced her small basement apartment with the small stone patio and the view of the Bay Area. She lived there for many years with Malice, the owner of the house whom Belle loved. Malice was a German woman who loved cooking for Belle and playing the piano. Belle's friends could not understand why Belle lived so meagerly, often urging her to move into a "real" apartment. Belle just loved the simplicity of the room, the beauty of the area, and the quiet of the area. From this simple life, Belle envisioned the house she might own one day; she pictured it either by water or among trees. Eventually, Belle would build her house on Martha's Vineyard.

Many years down the road, Belle still had emotional attachment to that time with Malice and their minimalist lifestyle. She believed that the simplicity and beauty of the Berkeley Hills led her through the process of finding and embracing herself. Belle continued to enjoy some of the same simple pleasures that she enjoyed at Malice's—reading, writing, studying, relaxing, and creating by the ocean or among the trees. In her comfort zone, Belle experienced an internal peace, deep breaths, and meditative thoughts and feelings. She found she was creating more, forming new ideas and coming up with strategies to accomplish those ideas. She designated a special area in her office as her dream and prayer closet. In this closet, Belle stored her new visions and therapeutic programming. She prayed for these dreams to come to fruition at the hands of God. On many occasions, her visions came to pass years later, accompanied by a path for their use.

Belle's experiences and transitions are not unlike those that anyone else might encounter. Achieving transformation and emotional freedom requires insight and the ability to reach deep inside to remove negativity; it requires the strength to deflect the emotional pain and fear that create the block, stop, and flat-line process. The deeper the traumatic event, the more difficult it is to release it. It is important to build, bridge, and combine these emotional experiences and remove any obstacles and obstructions to healing.

There are many forms of therapy to assist the transformation process. One such technique is emotional transformation therapy, which uses light, color, brainwaves, and eye movement to access unresolved memories and emotions within the brain. Another similar therapy uses EEG neurofeedback, which also accesses brainwaves as well as the amygdala—the part of the brain where we experience emotions. Eye movement desensitization reprocessing therapy accesses and processes traumatic memories. Many forms of psychotherapy are also effective, such as cognitive behavioral therapy, dialectical behavioral therapy, and other traditional forms of psychotherapy.

Emotional transformation is a process. It is not a single-step resolution. You must understand the importance of using the 5-Key System to direct you toward emotional freedom. The *Emotional Detox Journal and Guide* was created to allow a process of entry into influential emotional memories and content. The visualization aspect of the system is of most importance; it is the vehicle that will allow access to these memories and provide the blocks to build, bridge, and combine them into healthy tools. Once you have sorted through your memories and have made the decision to reverse the negative pieces, you will have created the conduit for transformation.

> *I was fifteen years old when I met Dr. Celina. She met me at a time of my life where I was desperately feeling confused and lost. I wore a beautiful mask and used my intelligence and friendliness to cover my pain. At sixteen years old, I was finally able to begin to rid myself of my past painful memories and was seeking to divorce my mother from being my parent. I began to have memories of being molested and later raped; this scar was the deepest and most painful. My family was dysfunctional; my mother used alcohol and drugs, my father abandoned me, and my mother's female significant other seemed to turn my mother against me and my sister. So I left, I moved out. I did not know where I was going, but I did know that I had to find myself. I lived from age sixteen to eighteen with various family and friends. I competed high school, and Dr. Celina helped me to acquire a certified nursing assistant certification. This helped me to become more independent, find work, and eventually my own apartment. Now at twenty-one years of age, I have found myself thanks to Dr. Celina. I worked many years in nursing homes, and now I am working in a hospital as a technician. My dream and goal is to become a registered nurse.*
>
> *Dr. Celina, thank you for being there for me and helping me to find myself and not get lost in the ways of today's youth. I thank you for believing in me and being consistently involved in my life transformation.*

Again, transformation is a process that takes on many forms and processes. We all have a story to tell, and it is in our best interest to tell these stories honestly. We get to decide which story ingredients will be consumed, and which will be thrown out. Once we have decided on the recipe for emotional balance and freedom, we should be aware of how these ingredients will mix, separate, or combine, and how they will impact our emotional performance. Remember that transformation opens doors; it establishes an environment of gratitude, internal excitement, new emotional material, and a sanctuary of emotional freedom.

Recently an eighteen-year-old girl—quiet, unpretentious, articulate—came into my scope and is now part of the Building Pool. (The Building Pool is a strength-based coaching process that uses the 5 Keys to Oneness.) Her writing strengths are incredible, and her insights are deep. She is sure to succeed as an author destined for transformation. She is currently telling her story through writing. The intensity of her lifelong plague is remarkable; when you encounter her soft demeanor, quiet voice, keen listening ability, and embracing smile, you would never image her relationship with strife. Here is her tribute to our first meeting:

A Soul Capable of Transforming

The raw muscle residing in my chest, palpating between breaths, barely clinging to a miserable routine...life. Entrapped in a world of self-loathing and discombobulation, the chaos would eventually obliterate everything in its wake. We'd been abandoned by fate, hope, and patiently declined any further inquiries and any others were long gone. The only ways up and out had suddenly vanished, leaving no trace. Sinking deeper into this crazed depression that left me alone, forgotten, cold....All whilst this monsoon occupied, destroying the dynamic and altering. I couldn't lay my finger on it. It was cosmic, almost supersonic. I'm able to recall minute details—the blinding light, the melody of pacifism. A woman's voice in the distance; unable to decipher, I followed it. I'd never felt so at ease with something, someone whom I knew nothing about, whom I wasn't sure was even real. She emerged, presented in an angelic state. I felt comfort within her eyes, such ease in her words. Her soul so pure that even her presence caused a sunrise in this degraded place. A module for growth and I had only realized now that I had been searching for her my entire existence. Complete strangers bound for introduction, driven by fate, we'd found exactly what we were in search of. She came from seemingly anywhere and completely transformed my world.

The idea of a "helper" key in therapy is to find a professional person who relates to you and your process. It is important that whoever this helper is, he or she has a deep understanding of your challenge and struggle. Multicultural dispositions are a major component to the therapeutic process. Your professional helper should be culturally competent in order to understand this process. You must understand your needs and what uniforms can assist you through your Oneness process. It is okay to have a menu of helpers who are trained in various areas. However, it is also important that you consult one helper at a time. Once an issue is resolved, move onto your next helper. This will allow you to explore and experience complete healing and transformation. For example: if trauma is the issue, you should consult a trauma specialist, who will use any of the many trauma modalities and techniques (e.g., EMDR, tapping, EEG neurofeedback, CBT, DBT). After you have resolved the heaviest issues, you may then transition into specialty treatment, and later to a life coach.

Be creative in meeting your needs. This is your journey—you take responsibility for your successful and effective landing. Your passport to Oneness is to become mindful of your excursions; to deeply understand and realize the pureness of your itinerary; to plan your journey strategically and with emotional balance; to reserve and visit intimate locations of the body, mind, and spirit that transport blocking, stopping, and flat-lining freight; and to be thankful for the turbulence that made way for forgiveness. After reaching this calm after the storm, you will arrive at your transformation vacation destination.

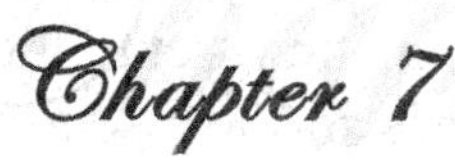

Victims of Traumatic Events:

Thoughts on Involvement in the Process

Trauma is an emotional response to a horrendous, inconceivable, or unexpected damaging event. These disruptive events can affect us physically, mentally, and on an emotional level. Their impact can extend to the creation of long-lasting emotional imbalances. Trauma presents in many forms and holds no boundaries. The impact of trauma is significant and has a chronic attachment to its victim. This presentation, whether minor or severe, can penetrate deep into the victim's psychological temperament. Even if an individual processes negative life events gracefully, trauma can leave internal scars. The subconscious tends to repress these traumatic experiences until a time when the victim is resilient enough to manage the memories. Victims who live with traumatic memories are at the mercy of intrusive thoughts and feelings that have a way of surfacing to create a conduit for emotional destruction. In many cases, the victim is not even aware of what the responses pertain to, and can experience great difficulty with self-regulation and emotional control.

In the case of traumatic events, victims—whether they have witnessed, been exposed to, or are an unwilling participant of the event—are deeply impacted in the form of life-changing emotional and mental health complications. The impact of complex trauma, or chronic exposure to trauma beginning in childhood, is horrific, consuming, and sometimes life-threatening. These complications can manifest as attachment and relationship issues, changes in behavior and emotional flow, dissociative and cognitive interruptions, health complications, or major mental health diagnoses. Trauma is a life-changing occurrence that brings lifelong influxes unless clinically addressed and embraced by working support systems.

Children ages five to eleven are most vulnerable to traumatic complications. They are of high risk because the imprint of these events can be overwhelming. Following a traumatic event, their development is negatively impacted by imbalances in their sensory regulation systems. They form internal disconnects and live in the mode of fight-or-flight. Unable to emotionally self-regulate, they exhibit uncharacteristic behaviors and moods, eventually developing an internal hyper alert–response system. It is easy for these victims to lose their self-esteem, confidence, cognitive skills, coping skills, and feelings of hope. Instead, these get replaced with, guilt, shame, blame, perception of fault, nightmares, intrusive thoughts, self-mutilation, victim behaviors, moods, and many other emotional and mental health-related consequences. Child victims are predisposed to depression, anxiety, panic attacks, post-traumatic stress disorder, dissociative manifestations, behavioral explosions, anger, sadness, fear, rage, or a combination of the above.

This narrative seeks to create programmatic foundations for these children and their families to help minimize the effects of trauma. The programmatic approach is to formulate a team of multifaceted and multitalented providers who will create varied programming vehicles to impact community healing and transformation.

If you have a history of trauma or have been diagnosed with a mood disturbance, your involvement in this process may cause an emotional imbalance and elicit even stronger memories and emotions. If you have a history of psychosis, this process is not recommended unless you are under the care of your psychologist or therapist. It is strongly recommended that, to proceed through this system, you utilize the private clinical support available through our Emotional Detox team or consult a clinician trained in the 5-Key System. If ever the material is too difficult to process or internalize, discontinue the process immediately and use only as a clinical modality with your clinical provider.

For those who are able to manage their emotional content, we continue to encourage you to maintain a support system and always have your support person(s) available. If you are able to journey through the system process without difficulty, it is strongly recommended that you take time out to relax in a safe place, possibly listening to soothing bilateral music or whatever helps you achieve a sense of tranquility. If at some point your emotional video content becomes too disturbing, use your internal remote to change, pause, or stop the video; write down the feeling, then debrief with someone, preferably a professional. The goal is to reach a "0" level of cleansing.

Chapter 8

THOUGHTS AND INSPIRATIONS

This section was inspired by the T.D. Jakes International Pastors and Leadership Conference 2016.

Much too often, we live in the darkness of past negative experiences, emotions, and thoughts. We forget how to shift and use these memories to our benefit. We start to believe that curses of the past have been put in our paths in a stroke of divine vengeance. This vengeance does exist, but only in our perceptions and our lack of intra-connection. We hinge on the edge of these experiences and allow them to block, stop, and flat-line our existence. The good news is, this is simply a preparation chamber for the next stage in our development! Eventually, preparation teams up with new expectations to build our destiny bridge. As we heal and gain wisdom, the destiny bridge leads us into the land of completeness and clarity; it is here that we find total immersion and purpose.

When we evaluate our Life Lines—links of connectivity and growth—we examine the roots, learn about the power of the stem, and wait and watch for the magnificent bloom. What is rooted is not always connected; sometimes the roots become rotten and other times they grow deep and strong to form a massive network. The stem is strengthened by the healthiness of the root, and the bloom depends on the roots' ability to connect to the stem. If the stem is weak, the bloom is small. However, if the root is solidly burrowed and massively connected, then the stem is strong and the bloom magnificent. The process of preparation can suffocate root growth and stifle connectivity. Preparing for transition and transformation can be very painful. But we must remember…without pain, there is no glory. This is the reward of persevering through the preparation stage.

If we can endure through the preparation process, understand its protocols, be clear about its intentions, and bridge deceptions to completions, we can then form and build a solid, connected, and rooted Life Line. The gifts that follow preparation to completion are enormous. All that you have endured becomes your strength, capability, and purpose. You take from the past, bring it into the present, bridge it into your dreams, and watch them grow and glow. Your roots are no longer stifled, nurturance occurs, and growth begins. No longer lurking on the threshold of darkness feeling scared and alone, you can face your emotional enemies, move forward without hesitation, and find resolution. Simply put: release it, fix-it, let it go, and keep moving.

When we move into completeness, it is important that we seek within ourselves a sense of transparency, unpretentiousness, loyalty, clarity, and wisdom. It is important that these characteristics be involved in our transition into Oneness. When our roots are falsely connected and we are opaque, we present with pretentiousness and grandiosity. Grandiosity shows a lack of character; it allows for unresolved internal disturbances to surface. It disallows long-term participation in any cohesive networks or systems. Your appearance, credentials, and articulations are not as impressive as your character, your exposures, your value, your connectivity with others, and your willingness to go deep into the trenches and work until it hurts. To be humble, honorable, and reputable allows for living with a sense of peace, dignity, and clarity. When we are focused and assured of ourselves, we soon learn how to do less with more efficiency rather than taking on more for grandiosity. We have to be aware of how we judge others based on their physical appearances. We tend to look for greatness in body size, skin color, hierarchy, and the presence of ranking symbols. When we do so, however, we misjudge worth and diminish each other's value, sometimes eliminating innocent bystanders' chances at success. Because of these shallow judgements, a morbidly obese woman, for example, will never sit at a board table. (*Men, however, often escape these kind of appearance-based rankings.*) When we overlook a person's interior because we are blinded by their exterior, we are shallow, superficial, and in need a reminder of our own imperfections. How can we create good connections with others if we have internal inhibitions that hinder our ability to relate to other human beings through shallow judgement?

Repairing the shattered pieces of our negative emotions that once consumed us is to find resolution for moving forward. Replacing these shards of memories with powerful, embracing memories of quality and substance opens the door to emotional sustainability. These sustainable memories become the backdrop of our basic functional mechanisms, enabling us to relate, attach, and manifest. Without these moments, we would exist in a dense fog dominated by darkness. It is important that we embrace these moments, for they are our Prozac; they are the monster glue that holds us together through the times of blockage, stoppage, and flat-lining.

When we realize the power of these memories, we visualize their value and allow our emotions to embrace us. This enhances the stability of our continual emotional flow, the purity of our thoughts, and the innate gifts and blessings that God bestowed upon us. In this state, we bask in our individual Symphonies in the Key of Oneness.

At this point in your transformation process, plan to give yourself permission to only allow in what you can digest comfortably without becoming bloated or gaseous. Ingredients to filter out are the silent behaviors that you developed during your Life Line process, such as being judgmental, disallowing greatness unless it passes your need for pretentiousness, having to be in total and complete control, and needing to manipulate situations. Create your Symphony in the Key of Oneness; open all the doors to your life and allow magnificence, splendor, and joy to fill your aura instead of than misguided perceptions and weaknesses.

Let's not forget that the emotional radicals that once had residency in your impenetrable cubicles have lived with you for years. It might be necessary to grieve their loss, and some sort of pre-grieving should take place during your enactment of the 5-Key System. To truly allow for this grieving process, the following steps should take place:

A. Release feelings of guilt and open your pathways to grief. When we hold guilt or are in denial of guilty feelings, we become blocked from proceeding through the grieving process. Guilt hinders us from feeling loss; it consumes us with questions, doubt, self-pity, and pain. This consumption compounds and creates new vessels for guilt to rein. We must grieve the negative memories that we choose to eliminate during the detox process. Many of those moments hold years of our memories. In many instances, these moments and memories connected the chapters of our life experiences. This makes them difficult to let go of. Emotional detoxing occurs when the guilt of cleansing these moments, memories, and experiences is released. This allows grieving to begin, and your transformation will be complete.

B. Release shameful feelings to open your pathways to grief and limit the impact of external interruptive blockers. Although through this process we rid ourselves of emotional disturbances, we still have family, friends, colleagues, acquaintances, and others who only know the old, untransformed you. Understanding and addressing your feelings of shame and installing coping strategies will enable you to face these old demons emphatically. When those in your life treat you as the old 'you', you can address them with renewed strength and certainty of your new transformational light. This will leave an impression of clarity without confrontation.

C. Forgive yourself. This is the healing process needed to open pathways to the grieving process. It is important that we forgive ourselves for our guilty and shameful feelings and learn to be thankful for their presence in our lives. After all, our preparations for tomorrow required the training we received from yesterday's troubles.

D. Find your faith. God provides us the vessel to travel through life; without faith, the journey can only go so far. For every action, there is a reaction. When you have depleted your ability to react, you can always count on God to refuel you for the next lap. Without a fall there is no glory, without pain there is no lesson, and without faith there is no transformation.

We are constantly in preparation for the truths and gifts of tomorrow. Be mindful today of tomorrow's introspective delivery blueprint. Where are you today? Is this where you will want to be tomorrow? Know that what you put into "you" today will determine what you will be putting into "you" tomorrow. Embrace the "you" that yesterday prepared for. Prepare for the truths and gifts of which you are so deserving. Create your own Symphony in the Key of Oneness.

Chapter 9

INTRODUCTION TO THE EMOTIONAL DETOX JOURNAL WORKBOOK

We all have a story to tell
it is time to rid ourselves of those stories
that hinder our internal growth.

This book and journal workbook were created as a support vessel for your emotional detoxification process. We are all laden with emotional toxins. Throughout life, in some cases beginning in utero, we are exposed to situations that compound and hinder our emotional growth. This hindrance impedes our characteristics, health, relationships, productivity, and in many instances, every aspect of our lives. These emotional intruders cripple our vision, handicap our expressions, and poison our ability to move forward. They have the strength to block, stop, and flat-line our every move and find ways to invade our every zone. We protect, harbor, and keep secret these intruders, masking who we are and suffering for who we want to become. We begin to adopt coping strategies that allow these emotional intruders to breed; before we know it, they have taken over and hold us hostage. Until we rid ourselves of these intruders, our bodies, minds, and spirits will remain in captivity. This is what gave birth to the 5-Key System to Emotional Oneness: An Emotional Detox.

Trauma is an emotional response to a horrendous, inconceivable, or unexpected damaging event. These disruptive events can affect us physically, mentally, and on an emotional level. Their impact can extend to the creation of long-lasting emotional imbalances. Trauma presents in many forms and holds no boundaries. The impact of trauma is significant and has a chronic attachment to its victim. This presentation, whether minor or severe, can penetrate deep into the victim's psychological temperament. Even if an individual processes negative life events gracefully, trauma can leave internal scars. The subconscious tends to repress these traumatic experiences until a time when the victim is resilient enough to manage the memories. Victims who live with traumatic memories are at the mercy of intrusive thoughts and feelings that have a way of surfacing to create a conduit for emotional destruction. In many cases, the victim is not even aware of what the responses pertain to, and can experience great difficulty with self-regulation and emotional control.

In the case of traumatic events, victims—whether they have witnessed, been exposed to, or are an unwilling participant of the event—are deeply impacted in the form of life-changing emotional and mental health complications. The impact of complex trauma, or chronic exposure to trauma beginning in childhood, is horrific, consuming, and sometimes life-threatening. These complications can manifest as attachment and relationship issues, changes in behavior and emotional flow, dissociative and cognitive interruptions, health complications, or major mental health diagnoses. Trauma is a life-changing occurrence that brings lifelong influxes unless clinically addressed and embraced by working support systems.

Children ages five to eleven are most vulnerable to traumatic complications. They are of high risk because the imprint of these events can be overwhelming. Following a traumatic event, their development is negatively impacted by imbalances in their sensory regulation systems. They form internal disconnects and live in the mode of fight-or-flight. Unable to emotionally self-regulate, they exhibit uncharacteristic behaviors and moods, eventually developing an internal hyper alert–response system. It is easy for these victims to lose their self-esteem, confidence, cognitive skills, coping skills, and feelings of hope. Instead, these get replaced with, guilt, shame, blame, perception of fault, nightmares, intrusive thoughts, self-mutilation, victim behaviors, moods, and many other emotional and mental health-related consequences. Child victims are predisposed to depression, anxiety, panic attacks, post-traumatic stress disorder, dissociative manifestations, behavioral explosions, anger, sadness, fear, rage, or a combination of the above.

This narrative seeks to create programmatic foundations for these children and their families to help minimize the effects of trauma. The programmatic approach is to formulate a team of multifaceted and multitalented providers who will create varied programming vehicles to impact community healing and transformation.

If you have a history of trauma or have been diagnosed with a mood disturbance, your involvement in this process may cause an emotional imbalance and elicit even stronger memories and emotions. If you have a history of psychosis, this process is not recommended unless you are under the care of your psychologist or therapist. It is strongly recommended that, to proceed through this system, you utilize the private clinical support available through our Emotional Detox team or consult a clinician trained in the 5-Key System. If ever the material is too difficult to process or internalize, discontinue the process immediately and use only as a clinical modality with your clinical provider.

For those who are able to manage their emotional content, we continue to encourage you to maintain a support system and always have your support person(s) available. If you are able to journey through the system process without difficulty, it is strongly recommended that you take time out to relax in a safe place, possibly listening to soothing bilateral music or whatever helps you achieve a sense of tranquility. If at some point your emotional video content becomes too disturbing, use your internal remote to change, pause, or stop the video; write down the feeling, then debrief with someone, preferably a professional. The goal is to reach a "0" level of cleansing.

Eoneness2x5K ∞

FIVE KEYS TO EMOTIONAL ONENESS

THE EMOTIONAL DETOX SYSTEM

JOURNAL WORKBOOK

CELINA BELMARCE PINA PSY.D.

INTRODUCTION

When our body is infested with toxic gatherings that are causing health issues, we immediately seek appropriate detoxing methods to eliminate these toxins. Just as we seek to eliminate these toxic gatherings for health reason, it is just as important to seek detoxing methods for emotional reasons. In our journey for oneness and complete emotional and physical balance, we must incorporate emotional detoxification.

We all have a story to tell
it is time to rid ourselves of those stories
that hinder our internal growth

There is an internal video that revolves through our mind and quietly imprints unidentified memories, feelings and emotions. This video contains an extensive history of our life experiences, many of which; we have chosen to forget, deny and repress. As these videos persist in capturing; events, experiences, blank exposures and many times unsolicited moments; an assemblage of the "Me" begins to evolve. Hence, creating the characteristics of the "You."

This journal was created to serve as a "Video Reflection Guide, a place to tell your story and a template to writing your emotional biography. This process will open your emotional cubicles and begin the healing journey through the "***5 Keys to Emotional Oneness; the Emotional Detox System***." This journey will lead you through the emotional freedom trail making five detoxification stops at cleansing, restoration, gaining emotional clarity, rejuvenation and transformation. You will journey from emotional obesity to emotional balance.

The viewing of your emotional video is to access the internal blockage, stoppage and flat-lining effects caused by memories that have accumulated in your emotional cubicles. Once you choice the cubicle (*memory closet*), your journey begins. Upon gaining access, begin to explore, depict, and understand the repressed memory. It is important to completely view this video until full understanding has been achieved. Take your time viewing and processing every memory moment by moment. During this process you have access to your internal remote (*to pause, stop, forward or reverse*). Following this exhaustive emotional process, it is necessary to find the cubicle, flush it out, and replace with a favorable or more understandable memories.

The objective of the journal is to promote healthy visual interpretations to telling your story. This guide and journal is structured and organized to assist in the process of detoxifying the emotionally clogged cubicles and ridding of emotional intrudes that plague growth and hinder emotional freedom.

The purpose of this guide, journal, biographical template; is to write your story and create your own self-help platform. A platform that allows you substantial emotional freedom to create, promote and publish your story. Through the pre-journaling exercise process you will create your "Global" story. This is your collection of biographical emotional data, historically gathered and written in chronicle order. This will create the platform for your processing though the "5 Key" emotional detoxing system. Once you have completed your detoxing process, you will have completed several chapters of your story, and will begin to experience emotional freedom and emotional transformation.

WHAT IS EMOTIONAL DETOXING?

Everyone has a story to tell and we rarely tell the whole story. This suppression of thoughts, feelings and rejected memories is the conduit for toxicity that blocks our emotional cubicles. Rather than excrete, dissolve, exercise or release these toxins, we tend to casually and conveniently bury these emotional intruders.

As we continue on our journey through the fantastical pleasures of the mind, that fill us with transitory bliss and random satisfactions. At some point, we stop to catch our breath and wonder why the shift in mood; why the need for superficial insulations; why the moments of complexity and perplexity. Suddenly in a glazing distance, a vision or feeling appears that seems somewhat familiar yet unknown and mysterious. We ponder this feeling trying to understand "it" then we let it go. Just in time for "It," the emotion the memory, to settle back into its well cushioned cubicle.

In many instance, the suppression of these emotional memories present as an indelible indigestion, which causes feelings of distress. This toxicity is unveiling and relentless and the stress is unyielding. The effects of these emotional intruders cause turbulence in every area of our lives. If these emotional toxins are not released, realized and detoxified; they will consume us in everything that we do. "It" will eventually become "You."

For many of us, it is relieving to allow "It" to continue to be "our little secret" or "our moment of wonderment or disillusion." As the journey continues; and knowledge, understanding and realization open the cubicles and the intruders emerge; "It" becomes and easier task to manage, control, filter, organize and create an emotional flow towards a stronger sense of emotional significance.

This being the incredible process into the detoxifying and transforming of emotions.

How To Use The Emotional Detox Journal

The following journal sections are to be used as templates. It is suggested that these templates are downloaded from www.drcelinaoneness.com to your computer, where you will have the ability to create your story in length and in privacy.

Journaling Sections/Templates

I. **Issue**: choice an issues from the Emotional Cubical Exercise: *i.e., Issue, Divorce*

II. **The Emotional Video Title** (*i.e., divorce of parents*); title, date and time of the entry

III. **Daily affirmation**: Create an affirmation for each entry, as needed.

IV. **The Cleansing process**: The Emotional Cleansing Key- The cubical opener to: Block, Stop and Flat line:

   a. The Visualization: Visualization I; Creating The Emotional Video

   b. The "*Emotional Balance Barometer*" measures impact of emotions related to the process: 0 no impact-10 severe impact

   c. Internal Balance Routine: relaxation exercise

   d. The Sensitization Key: "*The Body Sensation Barometer*" measures location of body sensations related to emotional processing of related issue intensity of sensation in the body; 0 no impact – 10 severe impact

   e. Impact of feelings (*sad, mad, happy etc.*), which feeling is impacting the emotional issue

   f. Internal Balance Routine: relaxation exercise

   g. The Release: for receiving Emotional Balance and responses

   h. Key written exercises

V. **THE RESTORE PROCESS**: The Healing Key; Forgiveness: receiving emotional balance

a. <u>Visualization</u>: impact of forgiveness

b. The "*Emotional Balance Barometer*" measures impact of emotions related to the process: 0 no impact-10 severe impact

c. Internal Balance Routine: relaxation exercise

d. <u>The Sensitization Key</u>: "*The Body Sensation Barometer*" measures location of body sensations related to emotional processing of related issue

   i. intensity of sensation in the body; 0 no impact – 10 severe impact

   ii. impact of feelings (sad, mad, happy etc.), which feeling is impacting the emotional issue

   iii. Internal Balance Routine, relaxation exercise

e. <u>Release</u>: Forgiving the memory

f. Written exercises

VI. **THE CLARIFY PROCESS**: The Wisdom Key; The Advent: New understandings

a. <u>Visualization</u>: Video or Audio related to feelings of trust and deceptions

b. The "Emotional Balance Barometer" measures impact of emotions related to the process: 0 no impact – 10 severe impact

c. Internal Balance Routine: relaxation exercise

d. <u>The Sensitization Key</u>: "The Body Sensation Barometer" measures location of body sensations related to emotional processing of related issue intensity of sensation in the body; 0 no impact – 10 severe impact; impact of feelings (*sad, mad, happy etc.*), which feeling is impacting the emotional issue

e. Internal Balance Routine: relaxation exercise

f. Release: Understanding of the painful memories

g. Written exercises

VII. THE REJUVENATION PROCESS: The Rebirthing Key; Emotional recreation: Bridging Passions and Mishaps

a. Visualization: reexamination of painful events bridging with preparation of new emotional growth.

b. The "*Emotional Balance Barometer*" measures impact of emotions related to the process: 0 no impact-10 severe impact

c. Internal Balance Routine: relaxation exercise

d. The Sensitization Key: "*The Body Sensation Barometer*" measures location of body sensations related to emotional processing of related issue

    i. intensity of sensation in the body; 0 no impact – 10 severe impact

    ii. impact of feelings (*sad, mad, happy etc.*), which feeling is impacting the emotional issue

    iii. Internal Balance Routine, relaxation exercise

e. Release: Bridging the negative exposures to innate gifts creating purpose

f. Written exercises

VIII. THE TRANSFORMATION PROCESS: The Emotional Oneness Key

a. The Visualization II: Documentary; the old me the new me.

b. The "*Emotional Balance Barometer*" measures impact of emotions related to the process: 0 no impact-10 severe impact.

c. Internal Balance Routine: relaxation exercise.

d. The Sensitization Key: "*The Body Sensation Barometer*" measures location of body sensations related to emotional processing of related issue.

   i. intensity of sensation in the body; 0 no impact – 10 severe impact

   ii. impact of feelings (sad, mad, happy etc.), which feeling is impacting the emotional issue

e. Internal Balance Routine: relaxation exercise.

f. Release: Bridging the negative exposures to innate gifts creating purpose

g. Written exercises

IX. Download from drcelinaoneness.com; forms to continue the journaling and workbook process. One memory will require many processing attempts before reaching transformation.

X. The "Note": please notate any emotional feelings/changes, unresolved memories, symptoms, flashbacks, moods, unusual somatic complaints etc.

Possible Need For Supports

If you have a history of trauma or if you are diagnosed with a mood disturbance, your involvement in this process may cause an emotional imbalance and permeate even stronger memories and emotions. If there is a history of psychosis, this process is not recommended unless you are under the care of your psychologist or therapist. It is strongly recommended that in order to proceed through this system, you utilize clinical supports, supports offered to you by our Emotional Detox team, or a clinician who has been trained in the " 5 Keys to Emotional Oneness; The Emotional Detox System." If ever the material is too difficult to process or internalize, discontinue the process and use only as a clinical modality with your clinical provider.

For those who are able to manage their emotional content, we continue to encourage you to maintain supports and always have your support person(s) available. If you are able to journey through the system process without difficulty, it is strongly recommended that you take time out to relax in a safe place possibly listening to soothing bi-lateral music or whatever helps you create a sense of tranquility. If at some point the emotional video content becomes somewhat disturbing, use your internal remote to change, pause, or stop the video; write down the feeling; then process with someone, preferably a professional. The preference is to reach a "0" system level. A "3" or lower is acceptable, but continue to process with supports to establish what continues to be the trigger. Perhaps it is a manageable memory. If it is a blocked or stopped memory continue to explore it. If you feel flat-lined, discontinue process.

JOURNAL WORKBOOK PROCESS

Pre-Exercise

Before you begin the journaling process, complete the following exercises: (*exercise begin on page 23*)

- Read and Create your "Positive Thoughts" List.
- List of Supports and safe/comfort places
- Image
- Key to Locked Emotions
- Key to Exposing Emotional Stories
- Key to Impacting Emotional Intruders
- Key to Emotional Cubicles
- "Internal Balance Routine"

Create your Global Story

Once you have complete the pre-exercises sections, you will write you "Global Story." Recall this is your collection of biographical emotional data, historically gathered and written in chronicle order. Once you have completed the "Global Story," you would have created your story guide for emotional detoxing. While following the "5 Key System" for Emotional Detoxing templates, you will refer to your Global Story. For in your Global Story, you would have organized and formatted your emotional journey.

As you journey through the writing of your Global Story you are apt to access deeper emotional memories and receive metaphorically symbolic images that may not be identifiable. Make note of these emotional indicators. Consider every feeling, every emotion and every visualization as important material. When these feelings and images appear add them to the story immediately, even if you have no idea of the meaning. Highlight this internal material to notate its unconscious presence.

From Belle's story, her Global Story would include every aspect of her emotional journey, the order in which it occurred, people who were involved, where these issued took place, and any other memories, as well as, any new images accessed. She would begin the use of the "5 Keys to Emotional Oneness; The Emotional Detox System" detoxing templates; identify her emotional imbalances at 8 years old. The separation of her parents. Remember the Global Story is just that 'the big picture'. It is not a detailed, point by point, rendition of her emotional challenges. It basically serves as the preface for the visualization exercise at the beginning and end of each detoxing key template.

For instance: Belle's "Global Story" would include each exercise in the pre-journaling exercises section. This section is the template for creating your global story.

The following as an example of using this section to create your Global Story:

Belle would begin from 1957, identifying the time and place and who was involved and any other memories. Then follow the pre-journaling exercises. She would include:

From Locked Emotions Exercise (page 25): Belle felt locked emotions of sadness, blame, pain, anger and grief.

From the Emotions Effects on our Body (page 18-20): These emotions often made her heart beat erratically, her stomach hurt and occasionally her breathing feel pressured.

From the Thought List (page 28): "Every emotional challenge offers an opportunity for growth."

From the Support List (page 29): The only person who knows everything about Belle, including her secrets and has been there for Belle for 50 years is Paula. She is her number one support person.

From the "Image" exercise (page 30), Belle would create her profile as how she sees herself today before beginning the Emotional Detox process. In the Global Story, Belle would create her current profile.

From Exposing Emotional Stories (page 31): All emotional barriers are listed in "A" then prioritized in "B" starting with the least painful to the most painful. In the Global Story these painful memories would be listed chronically from list "A."

From Impacting Emotional Intruders (page 31): Belle would recall her being hungry and eating rice pudding off dirty stairs. Next she would identify her emotions of feeling disguised that she ate dirty rich pudding and sad because at one point in her life she felt hunger. Her current emotional impact, is valued at a "4" because she still cannot eat rice pudding without this memory. However, currently this memory only provokes mild emotional stimulation, but because it continues to be an unresolved emotion it needs to be detoxed.

From Impacting Emotional Intruders (page 33): On this exercise, the emotional intruders from List "B (Priority list) is reexamined. Belle might have begun with the "**emotional intruder"** of divorce. The **"initial impact"** at 8 years old was a '10'; the **"current" impact"** is a '6'; the **"initial emotion"** experienced, was of withdrawal, depression and feeling flat-lined; the **"situation"** that caused these initial emotions was "father moving away." In the Global Story this would be delineated and emotions expressed. In Belle's 1957 portion of her Global Story, she would write about this impact and the fears she felt from the thoughts of losing her father. This would be further developed through the emotional detoxing system process.

From the Emotional Cubicles (page 34): Filling in each cube with an issues as outlined in the priority list "A or B" (page 26) then writing in the emotions affiliated with this issue will help to create your Global Story. These cubicles can be organized chronically or by least to more painful, or more to least painful. However, in your Global Story they must be chronically. This is a real good place to add all those new images and feelings that came up while writing your Global Story. For instance: When Belle was writing her story she continued to see images of big brocade flowers, she eventually realized it was an image of the chair cover that she used to sat on every day while looking out the window at the kids going to school. She later identified that chair as her "sad chair." When processing through the "5 Key" emotional detox system, she will elaborate on this emotion.

The importance of your Global Story is to serve as the foundation to creating you "Emotional Biography." The emotional detoxing process will complete this biography and create a platform for emotional expression. Perhaps you will use your story to help others.

Internal Balance And Safe Place

Begin each day by first developing an "internal balance" routine. Create a safe place that is calming and comforting. The purpose of this routine is to create a reflective vehicle that will allow you to cope with emotional imbalances. Your routine can include whatever helps you to relax and then return to that safe place for emotional balance. In this safe place, practice whatever techniques help you to stay centered. This may include: prayer, yoga, meditation, exercise, deep breathing and more. At the end of your journaling process, return to that same safe place and find you internal balance. At the end of your day, treat yourself to a soothing experience.

Journaling

There is no need to rush through the process, everyone processes emotions differently and every story has its own ending. So relax and create your journey. The Journal has provided one set of templates for each key system. Please, download templates to your computer from drcelinaoneness.com; Use the templates as a guide to your journaling.

"5 Key Emotional Detox System," Starting Point (page 36)

1. Chose an "Issue" from the "Emotional Cubical" exercise and write it next to the word "Issue." Each issue will be the thread for the system process. Once all 5 keys are completed and transformation has been achieved, the next issue will commence. This is the process for where your story begins and changes takes place. Remember it may take many attempts to complete on memory.

2. Fill in the Date and Time for each recording.

3. System Affirmation: Create your system affirmation, change as desired. It is important that you create an affirmation that fits your moment. Hold on to it as long as applicable, repeat it frequently, embrace it, and believe it.

4. Each Key segment will ask for Sensitization responses; the intensity of the body sensations, a barometer reading 0-10 ("0" less severe) and an "Internal Balance Routine."

5. Each Key has one or more exercises attached and blank note form for making notations

I. CLEANSING KEY

Visualization I

a. Now it is time to create your visual journey. Feel free to document this journey in this journal using these templates on your private computer or create your own visual or audio recordings. If you chose to use other forms of recording, be sure to include the information from "starting point."

b. Begin by softly repeating the issue, i.e., divorce; capture the visions that appears and feel the internal impact of those thoughts.

c. Continue to softly repeat the issue and begin to visualize and record the images, then organize the flow of the visions to create a story then create the story content. Write your story!

d. Replay the video until you have exhausted the script and all has been edited and ready for distribution.

e. Once you are comfortable that the entire story has been recorded and there are no rushes of feelings or images, bring the story to an end with a positive thought, feeling, or affirmation.

f. Throughout the visualization; Document on "Emotional Balance Barometer" the initial impact of these feelings. "0 no impact – 10 severe impact." Document in "Notes" the physical sensations experienced in the body that occurred throughout the "Visualization" process.

g. At the end of each visualization processed, document on the "Internal Balance Routine" line the relaxation and centering modality used.

NOTE: Again, it may take several viewings before emotional balance is reached. DO NOT rush through the video, take in as much as you are capable of handling. When needed you can use your internal remote to, pause, reverse, and fast forward or stop the video.

Sensitization

a. This is the Body Sensation Barometer. In this area you will document the body sensations that occurred during the above process. Document where the emotion presented in your body, the intensity of the feeling (0 no impact – 10 severe impact) and the impact on your body (feelings, *i.e., anxious, depressed, happy, joyful*). Try to keep a log of these sensation in order of presentation.

b. The purpose of this area is to recognize the sensations felt emotionally in your body and the transitions of these sensation throughout the process. This area is also used as a plateau for managing these emotional intruders and measuring the effectiveness of the process. Throughout the process these sensations will create a forum for improved emotional balance.

II. RESTORE KEY

Healing for Emotional Balance

a. Here you will document the release of the toxic emotions and memories, write about the process that occurred, what was learned and what was forgiven. You will develop coping mechanisms that will be useful to block and stop future intrusions. You will begin to rewrite you story. In rewriting your story try to focus on the positives and the strengths gained from the emotional detox cleanse.

b. Here you will document your ability to confront and forgive the emotions being elicited. Write a lengthy statement, specific to the issue being addressed. This is the healing area where you should access the true and pure feelings of forgiveness. Who do you forgive, what situation are you forgiving, what are you forgiving and how do you know all is forgiven.

c. This is the area where you will begin to plan and process your evacuation of the intruders and claim your release!

NOTE: You will experience the impact of the "Restore Key" once you have closed the issue cubicle and the emotional scale of 0 to 10 is under 3. This is the process of detoxification of emotional intruder.

III. Clarity Key

Wisdom from Deceptions

a. Here you will document your walk towards receiving and understanding the value of emotional wisdom. This is the "Aha" moment to understanding how all things are possible. This is the passage to solidifying your internal coping mechanisms towards sustainability.

b. The Clarity Key is the key to emotional evolution. This is where emotional consciousness and unconsciousness begins to make shifts. The emotional cubicles begin to, process, modify and evacuate the lingering infestation of the patristic organisms who have been embedded in the hollows of our emotional cubicles.

c. This is the area where the cubicles easily access the emotional stoppers, blockers and flat-liners, here, they reach full understanding and appreciation for their journey together. This bridging creates the path towards wisdom, and wisdom creates the path towards; pure understanding, discernment, forbearance and emotional balance.

NOTE: Once you honestly and succinctly process through those deep embedded cubicles and release those stubborn intruders; you will experience clarity, emotional wisdom and emotional balance.

IV. Rejuvenation Key

Rebirthing…Through Bridging Passions with Mishaps

a. Here you will examine the purpose of the past memories, events, and experiences that have impacted your emotional development. This is where you will surgically assess the evolvement of these events.

b. The Rejuvenation Key is important to the understanding of the impact these events had on you currently. This is where we look at how we were being prepared and strengthen for who we are today.

c. This is the key where we begin to understand how our innate gifts, our painful mishaps and our passions bridge together for emotional freedom and emotional balance.

NOTE: This is a place where you will release all emotional attachments to your pain and look at this pain as a challenge that was needed in your preparation for the strengths that you hold today.

V. Transformation Key

Emotional Jubilation …Stepping Into Oneness

a. The second major Visualization will occur in this Key. Follow the same process as in the Cleanse Key except now you are visualizing emotional transformations and how these event have empower and strengthened you.

b. This is the final system key to oneness. Here is where we have reached continuity in our thoughts and feelings with complete understanding and acceptance of the past painful events. We have now transformed these events into a catalyst for success. We have recognized the negative and positive aspects of these events and have been able to create a platform of emotional competence.

c. The Transformation Key is where the emotional toxins have been excreted and emotional perceptions are vivid. This is where continuity arrives and complacency departs.

   d. This is where wholeness lives.

NOTE: This is where you are have received emotional truth and balance. You will begin to experience emotional freedom and pure understanding of current and future events. Your vision is clear, your ability to defend against other events is restored, and you are now able to see yourself in a new embowed and strengthened light. Blockers, stoppers and flat-liners are in control. You have created you "Symphony in the Key of Oneness".

How Emotions Effect Change to Our Body

Research has indicated that emotional volatilities effect our organs and establishes major complications for our state of health. Stress is a major variable that affects our health in many ways. Negative life stresses are the catalyst for many physical illnesses; but also provides us with the strength to cope with life circumstances. However, stresses that are not achievable tend to cause a negative presentation in our body, mind and spirit. Following are examples of some emotional imprints that cause vulnerability to our organs:

THE EMOTIONAL LIFE OF OUR ORGANS

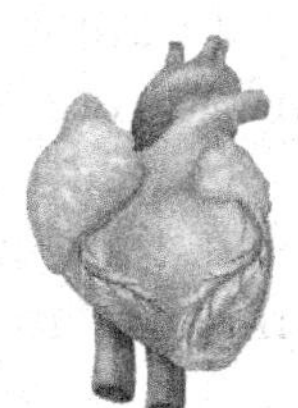

HEART: The heart, is a primary organ, it is very sensitive to emotionality. Explosive emotions like hostility, anger, extreme irritability, and internal torment; clearly effect the heart. However, those emotions that are less visible such as; loneliness, withdrawal, isolation, grief, and depression, also have an effect on the heart.

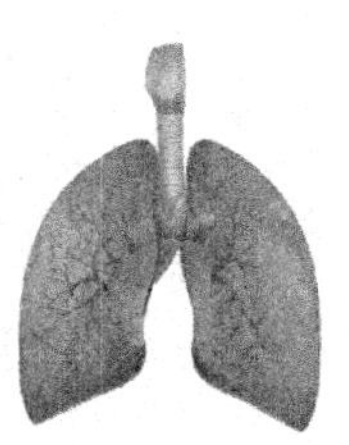

LUNGS: The lungs works with the heart and are as vulnerable to many of the same emotional conditions. Intense emotional material may create a constriction in the lungs leading to repertory conditions. Major grief, loss, bereavement; are catalyst for chronic respiratory diseases.

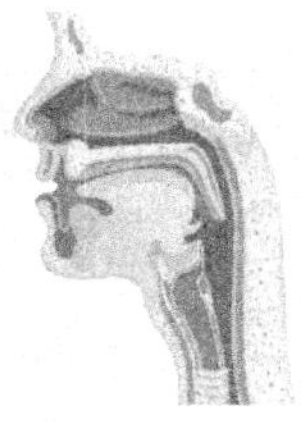

THROAT: It is notated that the throat is affect by not speaking the truth in extreme cases one may become muted. Feeling a "lump in your throat" can be caused by intense sentimental feelings.

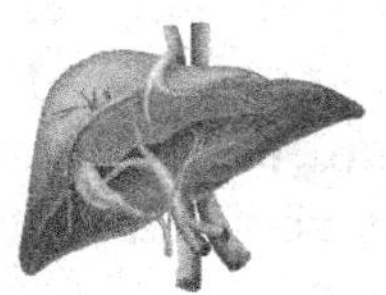

LIVER, GALL BLADDER: Both these organs are at risk of emotional influxes due to extreme anger, rage and other such frustrations or irritabilities. When the liver is overwhelmed with such emotions these emotions begin to affect the head with migraines, muscular tension in the neck and shoulders. These emotions tensions can also effect digestive functions.

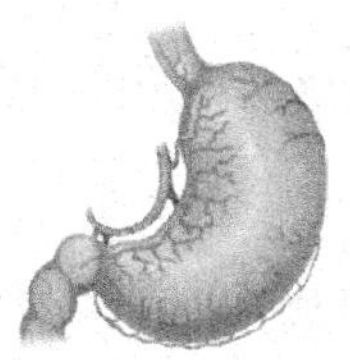

STOMACH: Harboring intense emotions like rage, torment, hate can lead to several stomach conditions. These conditions (*i.e., ulcers, gastritis etc.*) coupled with melancholic emotional tensions (i.e., anxiety, pensiveness, depression) can lead into difficulties with anorexia and other appetite disorders.

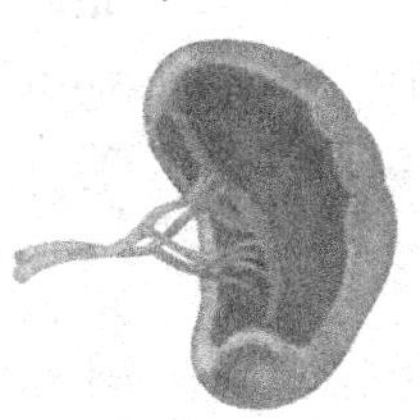

SPLEEN: When the spleen is effected by melancholic emotions the natural flow through the digestive system is distressed causing an agitation that leads to gas, bloating and other such conditions in the abdominal area.

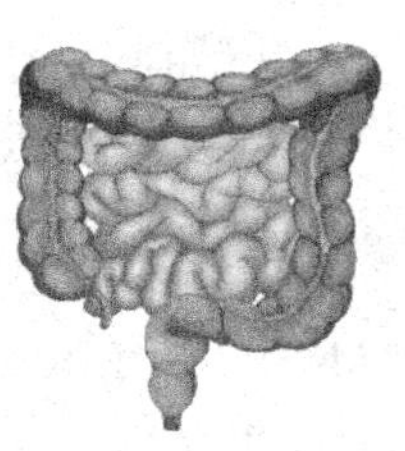

INTESTINES AND BOWELS: The intestines are often effected by psychosomatic or emotions that disturb the upper digestive system (i.e., the liver, gall bladder, stomach and spleen). When effect by melancholic emotions; the middle and lower intestinal tract can experience an obstruction in its smooth flow and function.

THE EMOTIONAL LIFE OF OUR ORGANS

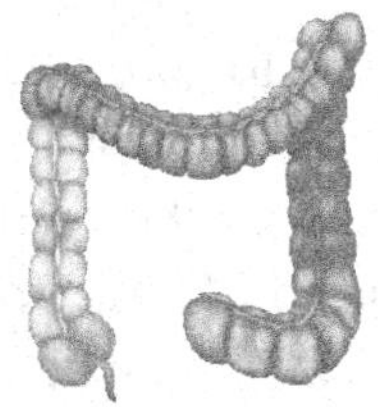

COLON: Excessive melancholic emotion (*i.e., profound feelings of worry, anxiety nervousness stress and emotional insecurities*) affect the natural functioning of the Colon. These emotional disturbances are the culprits for constipation, irritable bowel syndrome even colitis.

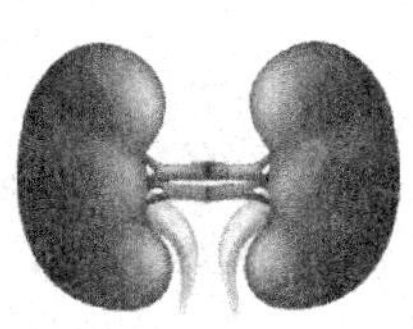

KIDNEYS: The heightened experiences of fright, fear and shock can cause extreme damage to the kidneys. These heightened emotions may cause one to lose of control of their kidneys and bladder functioning causing spontaneous urination.

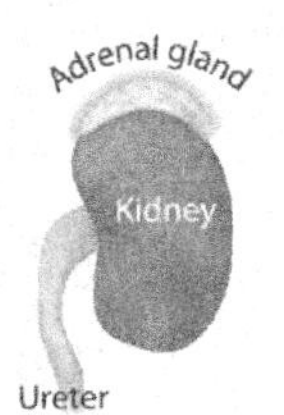

ADRENAL GLANDS: The adrenal glands, are affect by excessive stress. The fight-or-flight adrenaline response is triggered by a severe form of stress and emotional explosiveness. When the stresses are excessive and chronic they can lead to weight gain and elevation in blood sugar

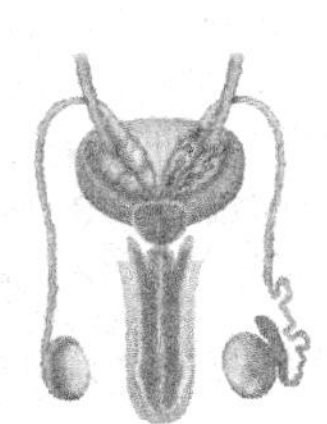

MALE REPRODUCTIVE ORGANS: Male impotence or sexual dysfunctioning usually due to a physical complaint can also be due to emotional tensions presented by feelings of fear, performance anxiety, insecurity and feeling inadequate.

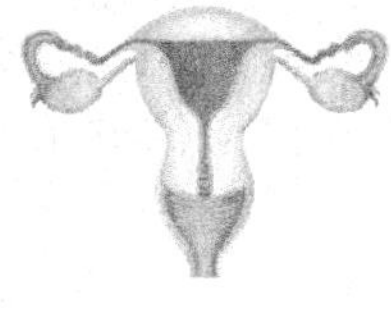

FEMALE REPRODUCTIVE ORGANS: Women frigidity occurs when a trust has been violated provoking feelings of anxiety and a shutting down of feelings.

Emotional Effect On The Organs

Liver and Gall Bladder	**Anger**
Heart and Small Intestines	**Joy**
Spleen and Stomach	**Overthinking or pensiveness**
Lungs and large Intestines	**Grief**
Kidney and Bladder	**Fear**

Joy is obtainable when there is a deep connection to a selflessness and an internal cleansing creating a strong spiritual bond. The inability to reach these depths or to become enthralled with an overwhelming sense of joy can initiate anxiety and heart palpitations.

Anger is an intense emotional response to feelings of agitation, resentment, rage, and a strong response to a negatively perceived situation. This response creates an internal disturbance that initiates a loss of energy, high blood pressure and respiratory issues, headaches and dizziness.

Anxiety is a state of inner turmoil that is associated with excessive worry, fear and a generalized disposition of overwhelming visual, sensory, and emotional perceptions. These presentations creates difficulty with shortness of breath, heart palpitations, fight-and-flight, ulcers and other complications that affect the stomach, spleen, large intestine and lungs.

Grief is an inward emotion expressing a sadness that is internally crippling, mourning is the outward expression together grief can cause difficulties in the lungs, respiratory system and create a barrier for energy to circulate throughout the body.

Pensiveness is an emotion expressing excessive thinking and melancholy. The excessive and deep involvement in thought coupled with the intense sadness or depressive feeling affect our spleen and create a lethargic presentation. The stomach is also affected with bouts of gas, distension and bloating.

Fear is the emotional response to danger. Fear is an internal alert for self-protection. Fear affects the kidney, bladder and involuntary urination.

Fright is a sudden intense emotion of unexpected threat. Fright has an immediate effect on the heart, and can also affect the kidney.

PRE-JOURNALING
EXERCISES
TEMPLATES

Locked Emotions

IDENTIFY THE EMOTIONS THAT ARE LOCKED IN YOUR BODY

Emotions that take residence in our soul and spirit. They create internal cubicles and compartments. They become occupants that are in need of eviction.

Circle the emotions that have taken residence and identify the organ that is effected (*i.e., Isolation affects the heart*)

BLAME PAIN RESTRICTIONS SADNESS

SECRETS RESENTMENT STRESS INSECURITY

HATE DISTRESS RAGE VACANT

INTIMIDATION DEPRESSION FEAR ANXIETY

AGGRAVATION TORMOIL SHAME LOSS

MELANCHOLIC QUILT ABUSE TENSION

HOPELESSNESS OVERWHELMED ANGER

WITHDRAWAL MOODINESS ISOLATION

CONSTRICTION VULNERABILITY

POSITIVE THOUGHTS

"ONE CUT TOO DEEP: WHEN FEELINGS ARE JUST NOT ENOUGH"
BY CELINA PINA SHEMO, PSY.D.

As you embark upon this journey, know that you are not alone. The following "Thoughts" were expressed by High School female students who have experience trauma and participated in self-mutilating activities.

1. Never smile for less always go for greater.

2. The most important things to remember is to have Faith in God and depend upon yourself.

3. Feeling safe really needs to come from within, we cannot always depend on others to make us feel beautiful.

4. Part of life's experiences are to learn how to navigate; most oceans have turbulent waters, eventually we will rest on a sandy shore or be washed out to sea.

5. Tell someone about the pain, someone who can help you process; it is much easier than a life time of living as a victim.

6. Need to control your own pain, by using other options.

OTHERS THOUGHTS:

- ***Maya Angelou***: *"This is my time to be me. I want to experience every good thing.*
- ***Keller***: *"Character cannot be developed in ease and quiet. Only through experience of trail and suffering can the soul be strengthened, vision cleared, ambition inspired, and success achieved."*
- ***Oprah Winfrey***: *"Turn you wounds into wisdom."*
- ***Celina Pina Shemo***: *"You must experience pain in order to experience purpose."*

- ***Kenji Miyazawa***: "*We must embrace pain and burn it as fuel for our journey.*"
- ***Napoleon Hill***: "*Every adversity, every failure and every heartache carries with it the seed of an equivalent or a greater benefit.*"
- ***Will Smith***: "*Stop letting people who do so little for you control so much of your body, feelings and emotions.*"

Create Your Own "Thoughts" List

Before you embark upon this journey create your own "positive thoughts" list

What are your insights and coping strategies?

For Example: Every pain creates a new melody.

SUPPORT PERSON(S)

A ONENESS TEAM MEMBER CAN BE REACHED BY EMAIL AT:
EMOTIONALHEALTH@DRCELINAONENESS.COM

NAME	CONTACT	RELATIONSHIP	EMAIL
Oneness Team	*508-696-4800*	*Oneness Mentors*	*emotionalhealth@drcelinaoneness.com*

My Safe Place (*beach, garden etc.*): ______________________

____

My internal balance routine (*yoga, music etc.*): ______________

____

____

IMAGE

I SEE MYSELF TODAY *(INSERT NATURAL PHOTO OF SELF)*

Picture of yourself here Date: ______________

Create your Profile, of who you are today and how you see yourself.

I am....______________________________

I am good at....______________________________

Not so good at....______________________________

Strengths....______________________________

Weaknesses....______________________________

I am liked because of....______________________________

I am not liked because of....______________________________

I am best when....______________________________

I am not at my best when....______________________________

KEY TO EXPOSING EMOTIONAL STORIES

LIST AND PRIORITIZE FROM MILD TO INTENSE
(SCALE 0 MILD – 10 INTENSE)

A: List issues as they come to you *(i.e., Divorce, bullied, beaten)*	**B: Prioritize issues from Column A** ***(Least painful to most painful)***
1.	1.
2.	2.
3.	3.
4.	4.
5.	5.
6.	6.
7.	7.
8.	8.
9.	9.
10.	10.
11.	11.
12.	12.
13.	13.
14.	14.
15.	15.

Key To Impacting Emotional Intruders

From Column B of "Key to Exposing Emotional Stories"

Create your Impact list

0 mild – 10 intense

For example: Belle ate rice pudding off dirty stairs: She was not hurt but disgusted by the act and thought of being that hungry. Belle continues to be disgusted by this event and it causes feeling(s) of sadness to think that she actually experienced hungry. Her current emotional Impact is at a "4."

Key To Impacting Emotional Intruders

From Column "B" of "Key to Exploring Emotional Stories"
Create your Impact List
0 Mild impact – 10 Intense Impact
Include encrypted emotion(s) of: Blocked, Stopped, Flat-lined

EMOTIONAL INTRUDERS	INITIAL IMPACT	CURRENT IMPACT	INITIAL EMOTION	SITUATION
Separation of parents	10	**6**	Withdrawn, depressed, flat-lined	Father moved away

EMOTIONAL CUBICAL

Write the main issue in the Cubicles below and fill the area with the appropriate aligned feelings, for instance:

DIVORCE
Anger, sadness, fear, death, empty, loss, lost, missing, isolated, depressed, lonely, withdrawn, left out

From the "***Key to Impacting Emotional Intruders List A or B***"; create each cubicle:

RELAX . . . DEEP BREATH . . . TAKE A BREAK

BE SURE TO FIND RELAXATION AFTER EACH EMOTIONAL WORKOUT

Relaxation techniques help in the following areas:

- Your heart rate decreases
- Breathing becomes slower and deeper
- Blood pressure drops or stabilizes
- Your muscles relax
- Your body begins to heal

Remember to access these or other relaxation, methods of your choice, daily to help with the healing process, this is to be recorded in the "Internal Balance Route:"

- Deep Breathing
- Yoga
- Massage
- Music
- Art
- Walking/Jogging
- Swimming
- Dance
- Gardening/Fishing/Boating
- Meditation
- Exercise
- Repetitive Prayer
- Guided Imagery

Create your Relaxation Guide:

- Morning Rising
- Mid-day
- Evening Calming

BEGIN YOUR EMOTIONAL DETOX JOURNEY

REMEMBER:

- Read the "**5 Keys to Emotional Oneness, The Emotional Detox System**" book first.
- Download all templates to your private computer
- Read the entire journal workbook instructions and understand the Emotional Detoxing Process as outlined.
- Complete the "***Pre-Journaling Process***"
- Create your "***Global Story***"
- Develop you "***Internal Balance***" routine
- Identify your support person(s)
- Begin the 5 Keys to Emotional Detox process
- Any Questions or concerns contact a "***OnenessTeam***" member at: **emotionalhealth@drcelinaoneness.com**

Journaling & Workbook Process

VISUALIZATION I PROCESS

CLEANSE KEY: THE CUBICAL OPENER TO; BLOCK, STOP AND FLAT-LINE

ISSUE: ______________________________

EMOTIONAL VIDEO TITLE: ______ **Date:** ______ **Time:** ______

MY AFFIRMATION FOR TODAY: ______________________________

Visualization I: Creating the Emotional Video (remember you have already built the foundation for this key in you "*In your Global Story.*" process at deeply as possible, capture every image every emotion.)

____

____

____

____

____

____

____

____

____

____

EMOTIONAL BALANCE BAROMETER: 0 to 10 ______________________________
(0 no Impact 10 severe Impact)

INTERNAL BALANCE ROUTINE FOR TODAY: ______________________________
(Yoga, Walk, Meditation, etc.)

A Letter To Myself

In this letter talk about the journey you have embarked upon, what you are feeling right now about this journey and where you want to settle. Address the video you have been viewing and what you learned about the situation, how the situation has hurt or helped you and how you want to resolve the situation and cleanse the memory. At some point in this process, also write letters to those individuals involved in creating the emotional blockages that have caused the invasion of the emotional intruders.

Date: ____________________

Dear ____________________

____

____

____

____

____

____

List of the individuals that I need to write letters to (*these letter do not have to be sent*):

1. ____________________
2. ____________________
3. ____________________
4. ____________________
5. ____________________

SENSITIZATION PROCESS

BODY SENSATION BAROMETER

THE CUBICAL OPENER TO; BLOCK, STOP AND FLAT-LINE

Body Scan and Location of Sensation: ____________________

____

____

____

____

____

____

____

____

____

____

____

INTENSITY OF SENSATION: 0 to 10 ______________________

(0 no Impact 10 severe Impact)

IMPACTED FEELINGS: ______________________________________

(sad, mad, scared, happy, etc.)

INTERNAL BALANCE ROUTINE FOR TODAY: ______________________

(Yoga, Walk, Meditation, etc.)

RELEASE

1. How did the release occur?
2. How are you feeling about releasing the memory?
3. What coping skill were installed?
4. How did your supports assist in the process?
5. What helped you to release the memory and bring closure to the story?

Response to above 5 questions:

1. ____

____

____

2. ____

____

____

3. ____

____

____

4. ____

____

____

5. ____

____

NOTES: FOR CLEANSE KEY

(VISUALIZATION/SENSITIZATION/RELEASE)

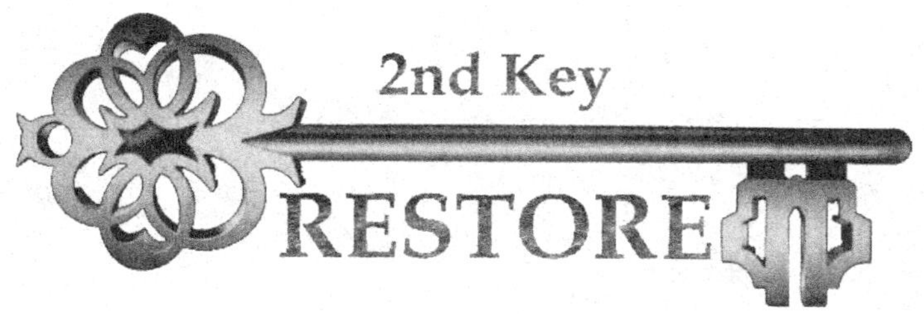
2nd Key
RESTORE

VISUALIZATION AND IMPACT PROCESS

RESTORE KEY: THE EMOTIONAL HEALING KEY

FORGIVENESS: RECEIVING EMOTIONAL BALANCE

ISSUE: ________________________________

EMOTIONAL VIDEO TITLE: ________ **Date:** ________ **Time:** ________

MY AFFIRMATION FOR TODAY: ________________________

Visualize and document the impact of the current issue, how forgiveness is found, who must you forgive and how has this issue strengthened you?

____

____

____

____

____

____

____

____

____

____

EMOTIONAL BALANCE BAROMETER: 0 to 10 ________________
(0 no Impact 10 severe Impact)

INTERNAL BALANCE ROUTINE FOR TODAY: ________________
(Yoga, Walk, Meditation, etc.)

Massive Emotional Blockers: Secrets

There are somethings that are just too difficult to expose. They can leave us feeling an intense sense of shame, blame, and internally broken. These memories are too painful to re-experience, so we bury them very deep in our unconscious. These memories are repressed to protect us from emotional collapse. They remain repressed until which time we are emotionally stable enough to retrieve them. The definition of repressed memory is: "The memory of a traumatic event unconsciously retained in the mind, where it is said to adversely affect conscious thought, desire, and action. It is common to consciously repress unpleasant experiences."

Do not feel consumed by your inability to access these memories. Jot down what you are feeling/sensing, about these memories that are inaccessible; then let it go. When you are emotionally able to address the situation, it will present itself. However, these memories may need the support of a professional. It will be helpful to your therapist to keep a journal of the feelings, thoughts, visions, dreams, and physical symptoms that these memories present. Remember that the "Note" area of this journal is a good place to make notations of the above.

These unobtainable memories are very often the cause of; flashbacks, depression, anxiety, phobia, delusions, personality changes, mood swings, somatic complaints and other emotional instabilities. As you continue through your emotional videos, become aware of these transformations. If these emotional instabilities are causing you difficulty, please consult with a professional to assist you through these traumatic experiences.

Meanwhile, know that you are empowered to accomplish your healing. You will take responsibility to stop the internal suffering and regain a sense of self and dignity. You will overcome these obstacles and be able to move forward. Now it is time to experience you internal gifts and passions and feel a sense of relief and wholeness.

EIGHT KEYS TO RESTORATION & HEALING

1. Tell your story, do not live with these radicals; let go of the pain. It is easier to experience the pain in the short term rather than as a lifelong lifestyle.

2. Forgive yourself first, finding forgiveness is the key that opens the door to the healing process.

3. Confront the internal turmoil and break down the walls that are holding you captive.

4. Recognize the truth of the events and process the event until all truth has been discovered, disclosed and documented. Do not fear accessing the pain, dig deep into your emotional banks and pull out all the emotional toxins.

5. Analyze and release the 4 emotional congestions, Fault, Blame, Guilt and Shame that have the capacity to block, stop and flat line. Reach complete understanding and realizations of these congestions.

6. Rewrite you story.

7. Install your self-discoveries.

8. Rebuild your empowerment platform and find your new positioning.

THE EIGHT HEALING KEYS

In this section, create your dialogue as it relates to one issue at a time.

1. Recognition of the issue (in as much detail as possible):

2. Access the related pain (dig deep):

3. Access the 4 emotional congestions and explain to indelible understanding:
   - Fault:
   - Blame:
   - Guilt:
   - Shame:
4. Evolution of emotions to full understanding:

5. Create a new "Me" visualization diminish "I am bad, I am damaged goods victimization syndrome."

6. Taking Responsibility for my perceived actions and strengths gained

7. Find Forgiveness: (*for the situation, those involved and yourself*)

8. Build an empowerment platform: (*Bridge your passions with your mishaps*)

THE HEALING PROCESS:

EIGHT KEYS IN CREATING A BRIDGE TO YOUR "SYMPHONY IN THE KEY OF ONENESS"

1. Create your dialogue from "***The Eight Healing Keys***" Have a deeper conversation about each issue, focus on expanding your story.

2. List the healings that occurred through the "***Cleansing***" process; *i.e., less depressed.*

3. Create a letter to yourself, regarding you healing process experience. Be sure to make note of the healing emotions that were strong and meaningful. (*i.e., Dear Me, I now know that what happened (name the situation/people involved)*) was not my fault, I am not to blame for this (*event*); I will not carry guilt any longer, and I will not feel shame for (*reason*), however, I will take responsibility for my (*action*). I have experienced a deep internal surge of relief, I am now ready to move forward from this (*repeat situation/people involved*) using my internal coping strategies of (*list the coping strategies*). Include in the letter feelings and experiences. This letter should be written after each event is addressed.

4. Create a list of understanding of the event, come to an awareness of the actions that occurred. This is a difficult task, move slowing; and, when needed with supports. It is important to see you vulnerability and create your platform of strength and power. Create your evolutional plan, "***The Me I Am Going To Be***."

5. Create a live video of yourself expressing your journey and evolution from the emotional contaminants. Create your recipe to success and coping. Remember that in order to heal we must replace those old images with the new restored images of purpose and value.

6. Create: affirmation list, poetic verse, dramatic renditions, or any form that allows for taking responsibly for the events

that occurred in your life. Not only the emotionally discomforting events, but daily life events; *i.e. with colleagues, work, family, friends, children. etc.*

7. Create a list of "Forgiveness:" I forgive _____(person(s) for ______(situation), deep in my heart and everything I believe in, I understand that _____ and I am ready to forgive and move forward.)) For each "Blocker, Stopper" situation, create this notation of forgiveness. Remember to search deeply into the situation and be intent about forgiving even the smallest of emotional experiences. Do not pass over an experience that causes a little cringe of emotion, address it so it does not grow into a more pronounced emotional intruder. This is the process of cleaning and healing in the emotional cubical that have stored so much negative emotional data.

8. Create your "***Symphony in the Key of Oneness***" story template:

   a. Heading "Healing" for moving forward. This is a skeletal key towards creating your success plan. For each "Blocker and Stopper" emotion, fill in your template with your success recipe, for example:

      - Name of Success Recipe: "Social Adequacy;"
      - List of ingredients for success in social adequacy; *10 lbs. of smiles, 3 tbls. of conversation, a pinch of warmth, etc.*
      - Conclude recipe with directions for preparation: *i.e., Mix all ingredient, stir softly with loving hands, and pour out to the world.*

   b. Once you have created your template remember the recipe, visualize its existence; body, mind and spirit, and reward yourself with a healing gift. The importance of this template is to have an accessible system of installing emotional data, creating a simplistic visual for coping and ongoing healing.

SENSITIZATION PROCESS

BODY SENSATION BAROMETER

BODY SCAN AND LOCATION OF SENSATION:

INTENSITY OF SENSATION: 0 to 10 ____________________

(0 no Impact 10 severe Impact)

IMPACTED FEELINGS: ______________________________

(sad, mad, scared, happy, etc.)

INTERNAL BALANCE ROUTINE FOR TODAY: ____________________

(Yoga, Walk, Meditation, etc.)

RELEASE

FORGIVENESS AND HEALING TO BLOCK, STOP AND FLAT LINE

1. How did the forgiveness occur?
2. How are you feeling about forgiving the memory?
3. What coping skill were installed?
4. What helped you to forgive the memory and bring closure to the story?
5. How did you find healing?
6. Have your forgiven yourself?

RESPONSE TO ABOVE 6 QUESTIONS:

1. ____

____

____

2. ____

____

____

3. ____

____

____

4. ____

____

____

5. ____

____

____

NOTES: FOR RESTORE KEY

(VISUALIZATION/SENSITIZATION/EXERCISES/RELEASE)

RESISTANCE

Dear Journal:

As I move through this process, I am beginning to feel overwhelmed by these feelings that I have worked so hard to bury. How can it be so difficult to revisit past memories; and so easy to put those thoughts, images and feelings away into their "do not open" box. I somehow feel consumed by these emotions and do not want to continue to remember them. But….yet I know that they are holding me back in many ways and I am feeling them penetrate my body and soul. How have I lived with this for so long? I want to detox my emotions, but it is so very painful. I wish there was an emotional detox suction machine that I could just release these emotional toxins into.

How bad can it be? These are things that I have experienced and want to release. However, I am still moving forward, although, there are times I experience physical complaints, mood changes, palpitation in my heart and internal rage or sadness. Perhaps, if I can just take one of these and eradicate the sensation, the experience, the change, and leave it in another box outside of my soul and spirit; then perhaps I could move forward with more ease.

Okay…..I am going to slow down, deal with the cubical that is holding me back, even if it takes longer than expected. I am an intelligent person and I know that in order to achieve internal success I will have to confront these intruders, reduce these intruders to a size of unimportance then leave them behind. I will not stand victim to myself nor to memories that have no importance in my emotional growth. If these memories are stifling my emotional growth, then I must find a way to unlock that cubical, keep the door open, until the cubical is cleansed then I can begin to restore.

I am ready to return to my emotional detoxing process, with all my supports in place, I will continue on my journey to total emotional wellness. I will list the three most problematic memories that I feel are hindering me from emotional success and create my plan to release/resolve.

INCIDENT	AGE	MEMORY	RELEASE/RESOLVE
i.e., Divorce	*8*	*losing father*	*Sadness and fear/write story*

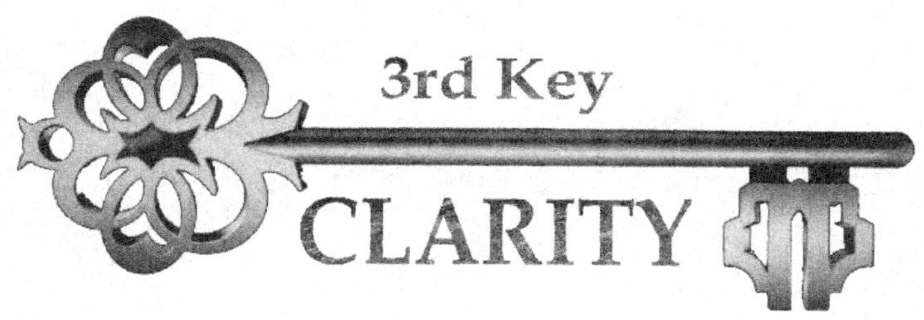
3rd Key
CLARITY

VISUALIZATION VIDEO PROCESS

KEY TO CLARITY: THE WISDOM KEY
ADVENT: NEW UNDERSTANDINGS

ISSUE: ______________________________

EMOTIONAL VIDEO TITLE: ______ **Date:** ______ **Time:** ______

MY AFFIRMATION FOR TODAY: ______________________

VISUALIZATION: Create a video or an auditory presentation on self-trust. What you trust about yourself, what you still fear that is deceiving about you. Record these thoughts and feelings. Remember this is just to assist in developing into a deeper sense of self. Do not fear being honest, for honesty and truth are important for reaching purity of heart.

At the end of this recording, create a clarity of thought collage (*in words, picture, poetry etc*). This collage should reflect your truths and deceptions. Then create a "Commitment" comment that relates to your deeper understanding of these truths and deceptions. For instance, I am committed to transitioning my way of____ to _____.

____

____

____

____

____

____

____

EMOTIONAL BALANCE BAROMETER: 0 to 10 ______________________
(0 no Impact 10 severe Impact)

INTERNAL BALANCE ROUTINE FOR TODAY: ______________________
(Yoga, Walk, Meditation, etc.)

RELEASING THE DECEPTIONS

1. Create your wisdom directory by making a list of your deceptions and how you will reverse these deceptions: *i.e., I lie to get my way but now I will divulge the truth to open my emotional awareness.*

2. Remove the mask: create a transparency script. This will involve your writing your story(s). This will allow you to see through indiscriminating eyes.

3. Evolving: Create a declaration of emotional evolution:

   I _______, do hereby acknowledge and declare that I will find emotional growth by _________. I hereby irrevocably undertake the oath to stop the behavior of ______________. I further undertake the oath of not continuing to allow the behavior of __________ to consume me. I hereby declare that I will continue to exhibit the behavior of __________________in order to achieve total internal peace, harmony and emotional wisdom and clarity. (Sign and date)

4. Seeing through a new set of eyes: Create your new story(s) through the eyes of wisdom.

5. Symphony in the key of oneness: Create a musical verse that you can hum or sing easily. Use this to elicit a calming and reminder of emotional clarity.

NEW BELIEFS

1. Create an "***I believe***" list: These beliefs should be create from an insightful and true understanding of the past emotional challenge. Explore every belief possible that involves the event. Your interest is in reaching complete clarity of the event(s).
2. Write a daily belief affirmation (*or repeat the same*) on sticky paper and place it on a surface that you visit often (*i.e., bedroom mirror, front door*). Read this affirmation an install it into your consciousness. Change the affirmations as new and deeper belief content emerges.
3. Create a Success Recipe Template: This template is for redefining purpose and internal data. For each "Blocker and Stopper," emotion that was identified in the Cleansing Chapter. You will fill in your template using each identified emotional challenge and create a success recipe.
    a. List of ingredients for success; *i.e. 10 lbs. of comfort, 15 lbs. of confidence, etc.*

    b. You will conclude with directions for preparation: *i.e., Mix all ingredient, stir softly with loving hands, and pour out to the world.*

Once you have created your template remember the recipe, visualize its existence; body, mind and spirit, and reward yourself with a gift of deep understanding. The importance of this template is to have an accessible system of inputting emotional data, creating a simplistic visual for coping and ongoing clarity on life challenges.

SENSITIZATION PROCESS

BODY SENSATION BAROMETER
THE WISDOM KEY

BODY SCAN AND LOCATION OF SENSATION: ______________

INTENSITY OF SENSATION: 0 to 10 ______________
(0 no Impact 10 severe Impact)

IMPACTED FEELINGS: ______________
(sad, mad, scared, happy, etc.)

INTERNAL BALANCE ROUTINE FOR TODAY: ______________
(Yoga, Walk, Meditation, etc.)

RELEASE

THE KNOWLEDGE AND UNDERSTANDING OF BLOCK, STOP AND FLAT-LINE

1. How did you gain full understanding of the event occurrence?
2. How are you feeling about finding full understanding of this memory?
3. What coping skill were installed?
4. What helped you to understand this memory and bring closure to the story?
5. Do you feel you have full understanding of the event and have received the gifts this event offered?

RESPONSE TO ABOVE 5 QUESTIONS:

1. ____

____

2. ____

____

3. ____

____

4. ____

____

5. ____

____

NOTES: FOR THE KEY TO CLARITY

(ADVENT/SENSITIZATION)

REFLECTIONS

(Based on the EMDR Concept)

Take a deep breath, create a soothing environment, use bi-lateral music (optional), close your eyes and visualize your safe place. Open your eyes, remain in your soothing environment and if needed, close your eyes and return to your safe place. When you are ready visualize your progress and success accomplished on the past several weeks of emotional detoxing: Make the following notes:

1. When I think of ______________________ (a situation); these negative feelings surface: ______________________, ______________________, ______________________.
2. The positive feelings that I would like to believe about myself are: ______________________, ______________________, ______________________.
3. When I visualize that video I feel the words that I hear are (circle level): False 1 2 3 4 5 6 7 True
4. When I reflect on the situation and the words the negative expression is ________________ and I am feeling ______________________.
5. On a scale of 0 to 10 ("0 being no bother and 10 being very bothered"); Right now I am feeling:

   0 1 2 3 4 5 6 7 8 9 10
6. And the physical feelings are in my _____________ (body area).
7. I have spent much time on this situation and today __________ (date); I am feeling from a 0-10:

   0 1 2 3 4 5 6 7 8 9 10
8. My new snapshot of this situation is ___________________

(Do not move on until the situation is resolved/manageable, bodily sensations have lessened, negative words and feelings have decreased and you emotional scale is "3" or lower)

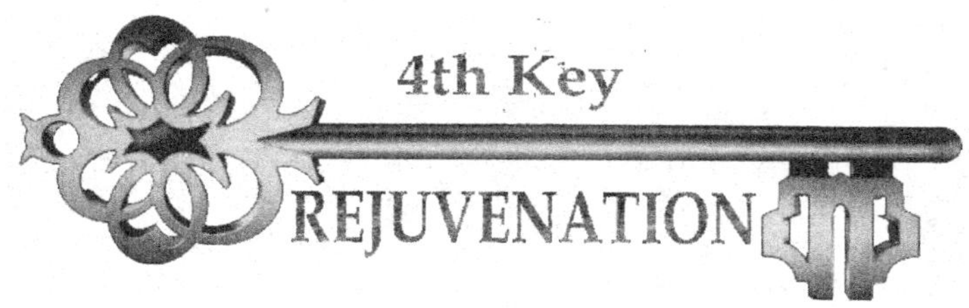
4th Key
REJUVENATION

VISUALIZATION REEXAMINATION PROCESS

REJUVENATION: REBIRTHING KEY

BRIDGING PASSIONS WITH MISHAPS:

ISSUE: ______________________________

VISUALIZATION: Reexamine the event, how can it be of substance to you today. Was this past event part of your preparation for today? If so, how has it strengthened and bridged your purpose. If not, how can you develop strength from this event?

____

____

____

____

____

____

____

____

____

____

____

____

____

EMOTIONAL BALANCE BAROMETER: 0 to 10 ______________________________
(0 no Impact 10 severe Impact)

INTERNAL BALANCE ROUTINE FOR TODAY: ______________________________
(Yoga, Walk, Meditation, etc.)

My Life

In each milestone create what may have been your passions and what events were mishaps:

	Passions	Mishaps
Birth		
Toddler		
Latency		
Adolescent		
Young Adult		
Adult		

Recognition Of Passions And Mishaps

List your Passions here:

____

____

____

____

____

____

____

____

List your Mishaps here:

____

____

____

____

____

____

____

____

List Your Passions On These Petals

LIST YOUR MISHAPS AT THE END OF EACH ROOT

THE "ME"

EVOLUTION OF PASSIONS AND MISHAPS

Using the pedaled passions and the rooted mishaps, write your story, in what ways did your mishaps bridge with your passions to create a more empowered and strengthen "You." Exam the passions and mishaps written above and describe how they have helped in revitalizing you. What are their connections? Why did they exist in your life? What strengths did mishaps bring to your strengthening your purpose?

HOW TO BRIDGE YOUR PASSIONS AND MISHAPS

List changes that can be made to Bridge your Passions with your Mishaps:

Past Negative Cause	Current Positive Affect
______________________	______________________
______________________	______________________
______________________	______________________
______________________	______________________
______________________	______________________
______________________	______________________
______________________	______________________
______________________	______________________
______________________	______________________
______________________	______________________
______________________	______________________
______________________	______________________

PRIORITIZE YOUR PASSIONS, YOUR MISHAPS, AND YOUR CHANGES

Passions	Mishaps	Changes to self

CREATE YOUR LIVING TREE OF CHANGE PROCLAMATION

I, ___________________________, proclaim to do the following in order to utilize the gifts and strengths bestowed upon me and to overcome the burdens that have disempowered me:

I AM:	I CAN:
______________________________	______________________________
______________________________	______________________________
______________________________	______________________________
______________________________	______________________________
______________________________	______________________________
______________________________	______________________________
______________________________	______________________________
______________________________	______________________________
______________________________	______________________________
______________________________	______________________________
______________________________	______________________________

RELEASE

THE KEY TO BRIDGING PASSIONS WITH MISHAPS, REBIRTHING TO MANAGE THE BLOCKERS, STOPPERS AND FLAT-LINERS

---

1. How did you gain insight into bridging the negative with the positive?
2. How are you feeling about the bridging of these memory?
3. What coping skill were installed?
4. What was your "Aha" rebirthing moment?
5. Do you feel you have bridged your passions with your mishaps to receive your innate gifts?

RESPONSE TO ABOVE 5 QUESTIONS:

1. ____

____

____

2. ____

____

____

3. ____

____

____

4. ____

____

____

5. ____

____

SENSITIZATION PROCESS

BODY SENSATION BAROMETER

BODY SCAN AND LOCATION OF SENSATION: ____________

____

____

____

____

____

____

____

____

____

____

____

____

____

INTENSITY OF SENSATION: 0 to 10 ____________________

(0 no Impact 10 severe Impact)

IMPACTED FEELINGS: ______________________________

(sad, mad, scared, happy, etc.)

INTERNAL BALANCE ROUTINE FOR TODAY: ____________________

(Yoga, Walk, Meditation, etc.)

SELF-EVALUATION

CONGRATULATIONS! You have toiled through very complex material, and you have succeeded. Now it is time to explore your success, accomplishments and re-evaluate your need for more support in eliminating the emotional toxins. In the Pre-Journal Workbook activities, you created your toxic cubicles, return to that exercise and list the memories that were successfully evacuated below and assess ("0" is no bother 10 severe bother; chose level 0,1,2,3,4,5,6,7,8,9,10):

Toxic Cubical Memory Addressed	Initial Level of Severity 0-10	Current Level of Severity 0-10	Internal Sensation *(list feeling/body area)*
1. ____________	____________	____________	____________
____________	____________	____________	____________
2. ____________	____________	____________	____________
____________	____________	____________	____________
3. ____________	____________	____________	____________
____________	____________	____________	____________
4.			
____________	____________	____________	____________
5.			
____________	____________	____________	____________

If you have not achieved an emotional scale under three (3), perhaps the memory is still in need of some processing unless you are feeling comfortable. If you have taken it as far as you can, do a body scan to reassess the magnitude of your bodily sensations. If you continue to feel discomfort, then seek supports that can help you access the remaining toxicity that is stuck or hidden. Continue to be aware of your body sensations to determine the magnitude of the remaining memory.

A Brief Thought On Personality Development

From the Book: "Strands of Silk,"
By: Celina Pina Shemo, Psy.D.

"***Strands of Silk***," is a look into defiant behaviors. Addressing how we perceive others based upon how they; act, look and respond to our expectations.

What has been lost in translation, is the inner most feelings of those who are feared as defiant, difficult to manage and entwined in a negative web.

"***Strands of Silk***" seeks to provide insight into those who live in these complexities; who are attempting to build reformation and restructuring in order to renegotiate life and living. Also, for those who have continued to be enmeshed in this web of entanglement, due to their unresolved inner turmoil. This is a population of talented creative and intelligent individuals; who are in need of learning how to feel, negotiate, and relieve their heart of confusions and their mind of negative images.

It is this author's belief that positive development of ego is critical to the development of a resilient personality. This development is based on the unknown factors and maturate into the realized factors. If the psychic, genetic and unconscious has not experienced a healthy history or development then the personality will meet difficult challenges in development. If the unconscious harbors unpleasant memories, but has healthy pre-development then the personality stands a chance for transitioning into healthier formations. If the ego and unconscious have not developed because of genetic deposition, early trauma, attachment and other developmental issues, the personality will be compromised and over-burdened. We need to cleanse the fragmentation of self and restore the ego in order to achieve clarity and rejuvenation.

NOTES: FOR REJUVENATION

(BRIDGING PASSIONS WITH MISHAPS)

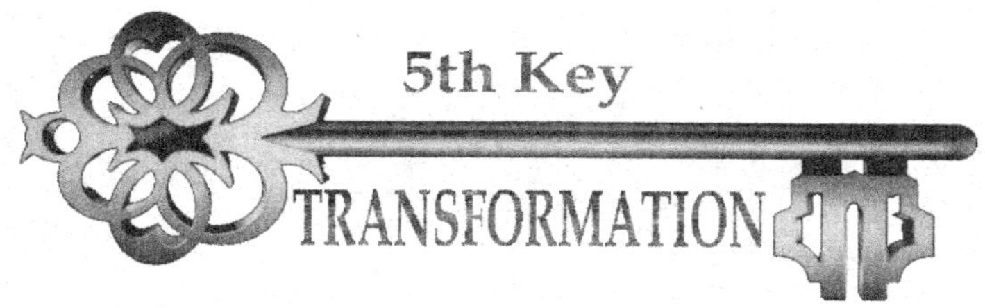
5th Key
TRANSFORMATION

VISUALIZATION II PROCESS

TRANSFORMATION KEY: EMOTIONAL ONENESS KEY

ISSUE: ____________________

EMOTIONAL VIDEO TITLE: ______ **Date:** ______ **Time:** ______

MY AFFIRMATION FOR TODAY: ____________________

Visualization II: This is the second major visualization. Here you will create a biographical live documentary depicting the past "You" and the new "You." Create your destiny. Visualize your new-found clarity and coping mechanisms. Acknowledge you healing and forgiving. Fully describe your rebirthing experience and how your past pains where for your preparation into today.

____

____

____

____

____

____

____

____

____

EMOTIONAL BALANCE BAROMETER: 0 to 10 ____________________

(0 no Impact 10 severe Impact)

INTERNAL BALANCE ROUTINE FOR TODAY: ____________________

(Yoga, Walk, Meditation, etc.)

Today: ____________________

Create Your Destination Into The Key Of Oneness

Dare to Dream, this has been an incredible journey. Your diligence and perseverance in accomplishing such a delicate and fragile task is commendable. Through this process, you have cleared away the vulnerabilities that were blocking, stopping and perhaps flat-lining you. It is now that you will begin to receive yours gifts. The key to receiving is to take hold of effort, add motivation and creativity and continue your walk in diligence. Be tenacious, this is your time for greatness to occur. The good news is that the heavy emotional baggage that weighted you down for years has been lifted. Now you can fly and take to the sky.

Congratulations! You have received you passport to emotional freedom. Enjoy you journey.

SENSITIZATION PROCESS

BODY SENSATION BAROMETER

EMOTIONAL ONENESS KEY

BODY SCAN AND LOCATION OF SENSATION: ________________

____

____

____

____

____

____

____

____

____

____

____

____

____

____

____

____

INTENSITY OF SENSATION: 0 to 10 ________________________

(0 no Impact 10 severe Impact)

IMPACTED FEELINGS: ____

(sad, mad, scared, happy, etc.)

INTERNAL BALANCE ROUTINE FOR TODAY: ________________________

(Yoga, Walk, Meditation, etc.)

NOTES: FOR TRANSFORMATION

(INFINITE CHANGE)

UNLOCKED EMOTIONS
(AFTER TRANSFORMATION)

Now that we have excreted, moved out, evicted those emotional intruder you have unlocked emotions to now experience a renewed relationship with self. Embrace your emotional freedom and explore the oceans of:

FREEDOM…AUTONOMY...EFFORTLESSNESS

HAPPINESS … OPENNESS … HEALING

CIRCLE THE EMOTIONS YOU HAVE UNLOCKED OR INSERT YOU OWN EMOTIONAL EXPRESSIONS

Relief Serenity Painlessness Peace

Wholeness Control Joy

Fulfillment Pride Relaxation Dignity Love

Security Safety Courage Forgiveness

Life Creativity Happiness Compassion

Clarity Passion Laughter Connectivity

REFLECTIONS
(BASED ON THE EMDR CONCEPT)

Take a deep breath, create a soothing environment, use bi-lateral music (optional), close your eyes and visualize your safe place. Open your eyes, remain in your soothing environment and if needed, close your eyes and return to your safe place. When you are ready visualize your progress and success accomplished on the past several weeks of emotional detoxing: Make the following notes:

When I think of ____________________ (a situation); these negative feelings surface: __________________________,
________________________, ________________________

The positive feelings that I would like to believe about myself are: ________________________, ________________________,
____

When I visualize that video I feel the words that I hear are (circle level): False 1 2 3 4 5 6 7 True

When I reflect on the situation and the words the negative expression is ________________ and I am feeling ________________

On a scale of 0 to 10 ("0 being no bother and 10 being very bothered"); Right now I am feeling:

0 1 2 3 4 5 6 7 8 9 10

And the physical feelings are in my ________________________ (body area).

I have spent much time on this situation and today ____________ (date); I am feeling from a 0-10:

0 1 2 3 4 5 6 7 8 9 10

My new snapshot of this situation is ________________________

(Do not move on until the situation is resolved/manageable, bodily sensations have lessened, negative words and feelings have decreased and you emotional scale is "3" or lower.)

How I See Myself Today

Picture of yourself here Date: __________

Create your Profile, of who you are today. What is your Self-Image?

A Symphony in the Key of Oneness

In the beginning, there was a miraculous transformation
An embodiment of color, lights and magnificence
A softness of touch coddled by sweet melodies

Then the leaves changed
And the colors
No longer brilliant
Now infiltrated with misdirection
Softness became harshness
Harshness turned to pain
Brightness lived in darkness
Singing a melancholic melody

Reaching for new beginnings
Reaching……Reaching…..Reaching
A small growth in the middle of a weeded field
Picking …Picking……Picking
Looking for the light, looking for the colors
Seeking…….Seeking…….Seeking
Finally a glimmer of light, a shading in the distance
New pathways leading from Density to Sparsity
Rushing forward into the Rhythm of living
Breathing…..Breathing……Breathing

Deep Breaths
Feeling release, Feeling healing, Feeling autonomous
Building……Building……Building
Growth from Darkness Returning to the Light
Bridging……Bridging….. Bridging
Past transformed from yesterday's gifts into tomorrow's purpose
Bridging Passions and mishaps into
A Symphony in the Key of Oneness
Arriving at destination….Emotional Freedom

DR. CELINA

CREATE YOUR OWN

"Symphony In The Key Of Oneness"

Use any creative media: song, video, drama, poetry, dance, spoken word, instrumental etc.

APPENDIX
THE WONDERS OF ESSENTIAL OILS

The following information can be found on www.godesana.com/drcelina: GoDesana Essential products "*are raw, plant-based functional whole food derived from organic and wild harvested sources.*" GoDesana Organic, "*is committed to providing proprietary products using pure, certified organic and wild crafted ingredients from around the world.*"

For the purposes of detoxing the emotions; GoDesana has emotional blends that are helpful for many emotional instabilities. The following are GoDesana emotional blends:

- Cherished Place
- Compassion
- Delight
- Dispel Anger
- Dispel Bad Relationships
- Dispel Entitlement
- Dispel Fear
- Dispel Judgment
- Dispel Poverty
- Dispel Self-Sabotage
- Dispel Sickness
- Dispel Victimization
- Dragon Fire
- Dream Weaver
- E-Motion
- Finishing Oil
- Gratitude
- Grief Relief
- Healer's Heart
- Humility
- Prosper
- Restore Reality Check
- Restore Courage
- Restore Empathy
- Restore Independent Self
- Restore Tolerance
- Right Use of Power
- Restore Unconditional Love
- Shaman Blend
- Terra
- Transform

Visit the Website for the Data Sheets on each Essential Oil.

About The Author

CELINA BELMARCE PINA PSY.D.

As a seasoned clinician, of 30 years, and a survivor of sexual, physical abuse and domestic violence, I have dedicated my life's work to helping those who have experienced a traumatic event. I have been in private practice for 22 years serving the minority and disadvantaged populations of Southeastern Massachusetts, Cape and the Islands. For many years, I provided forensic evaluations on sexually abused children. I was fortunate to have studied under an extraordinary team of professionals in the field of trauma. In 1988, I began my journey as a sexual abuse evaluator and later grew focusing exclusively on trauma. I eventually was recognized as a child sexual abuse expert witness in the Massachusetts court system.

It is my clinical belief that our negative life exposures, which can also be seen as our teachers for future successes, have caused an imbalance in our emotional growth, which attacks our physical health and the ability to progress into completeness. We are born with innate gifts that are consumed by these exposures and then they are placed on hold. It is important that we eliminate these toxins to receive the gifts that God planned for us. Once we are cleansed of these toxins we can then embrace our innate passions, take the strengths from those negative life exposures and journey into "A Symphony in the Key of Oneness." This is the key that creates our new life melody.

My clinical model is "Growth through Inner Experience." My belief that we must look internally for our healing, forgiveness and allow for pure expression of our pain. This is the key to finding emotional growth. Once those cubicles are opened and emptied, we are then able to create our paths towards oneness and purity of thought and actions. My clinical approach, is to affect healing from the inside through the use of various clinical techniques incorporating the creative, expressive and preforming arts.

I am recognized for my clinical insight, diagnostic proficiencies and my "out of the box" treatment modalities. Over the years, I have serviced families who now continue to refer their children and grandchildren. My practice has grown to include treatment for children (starting at 2 years of age) to all ages with a large population of seniors who are survivors of trauma.

"The 5 Keys to Emotional Oneness; The Emotional Detox System" book and journal were created to provide, those who are intoxicated with emotional tragedies, a vehicle to telling their story. This system is cognitively based, using creative modalities and healing processes for the elimination of past emotional tragedies, while creating a platform for coping and managing new entries.

In 1992, Dr. Celina, created a platform for helping those who live in pain. She is the founder and CEO of Venilia Gardens, Incorporated dba, Cultural Counseling Services, which is a 501 C 3, organization. The mission is to provide a mental health therapeutic milieu to the diverse and multicultural population of children and families in Southeastern Massachusetts, Cape and Islands. Dr. Pina is also licensed to provide these same services in New York State. Dr. Celina is recognized for her distinguished clinical abilities in providing diagnostic assessments in the area of trauma related issues. Dr. Celina also provides Colon Hydrotherapist and emotional detoxing services at Martha's Vineyard Wellness Detox Spa, where she is a part owner.

Dr. Celina is bi-lingual, in Cape Verdean Creole; sits on several boards, and published, "One Cut Too Deep," which address self-mutilation. She is currently writing a book on the growth of defiant behaviors as it relates to trauma, "Strands of Silk." Dr. Celina has hosted several radio and television talk shows throughout California and Massachusetts, she has served as a keynote speaker for several organizations and continues to deliver workshops, trainings and public speaking engagements to varying audience.

CPSIA information can be obtained
at www.ICGtesting.com
Printed in the USA
FSOW03n2131301017
40565FS